The Memory Book

The Memory Book

by

HARRY LORAYNE and **JERRY LUCAS**

STEIN AND DAY/*Publishers*/New York

First published in 1974
Copyright © 1974 by Harry Lorayne and Jerry Lucas
Library of Congress Catalog Card No. 73-90705
All rights reserved
Designed by David Miller
Printed in the United States of America
Stein and Day/*Publishers*/Scarborough House, Briarcliff Manor, N.Y. 10510
ISBN 0-8128-1664-1

ELEVENTH PRINTING, 1974

CONTENTS

FOREWORD: JERRY LUCAS

As a child, I had a peculiarly busy mind. I can never remember a time when my mind wasn't occupied with some sort of activity, whether it was communicating directly with someone else, or being actively involved with a mental game of my own invention.

By the time I was eight years old, I had so much nervous energy that it was hard for me to sit still. On lengthy automobile trips my constant fidgeting, tapping, and so on got on my parents' nerves. It got to the point where I became used to requests from them to "calm down a little."

Just after one such request, I remember looking at an oil company billboard and saying to myself, "What would 'SHELL' look like if the letters were arranged in alphabetical order?" I mentally rearranged it to "EHLLS," and I was hooked. Ever since then, I have memorized words alphabetically as well as normally.

Thanks to this mental habit, I could spell amazingly well as a child. If you can rearrange a word instantly and spell it in alphabetical order, you know that word very well. To give some examples: CAT becomes ACT, MEMORY becomes EMMORY, JERRY LUCAS becomes EJRRY ACLSU, and HARRY

LORAYNE becomes AHRRY AELNORY! Once I've alphabet-ized a word, I can remember it in that form—when you read the chapter on how to remember English and foreign vocabulary, you'll understand how I do this. I apply the same system, since an alphabetized word is like a foreign word.

I soon followed this alphabetical spelling game with various other kinds of mental games. You might think I was a bit crazy if I took the time to explain all of them, so I won't, but they did require a lot of counting, cataloging, and recall on the part of a very young boy.

As I grew older, my mental games and activities became more complex. I began to develop simple memory systems to help me with my studies in school. To me, schoolwork always seemed to be at least 90 percent memory work, and I wanted to make it easier and less time-consuming for myself. These systems worked, and I began to expand and sophisticate them. They worked well for me throughout junior high school and high school, where I was practically a straight-A student.

I would like to impress upon you that all of this mental activity was of a private nature. No living human being knew that I had the ability, for example, to alphabetize any word faster than most people could spell it normally, nor did anyone know how involved I was with other mental activities and memory systems.

An important change took place when I entered college. I read one of Harry Lorayne's books and used many of his systems or ideas in areas where I thought his were better, or simpler, or easier to apply; others I adapted to my own. He became something of an idol to me, and I was soon to find out how the combination of his systems and mine would help me in my college studies.

My roommate at Ohio State University during my freshman year was John Havlicek, the great professional basketball star of the Boston Celtics. John became the first person to know about all the things that went on in my mind.

My first college class was traumatic. I entered the classroom and sat in the back row, knowing other students would be unable to see over my six-foot-eight frame. It was an American history class.

The professor spent about fifteen minutes telling us what he expected of us and how the class would be conducted. His last statement before he excused us was something to the effect that "Any athlete who expects to be in my class, sit in the back row, do nothing, and get good grades is sadly mistaken. You are excused."

I told John Havlicek what had happened and shared with him my determination to use memory systems to my best advantage in this particular class.

"What systems?" he asked me, and it all began to flow out for the first time. I told John how I had begun to spell alphabetically as a child and I demonstrated it for him.

He couldn't really believe what he was hearing. I explained, as best I could, how my mind worked and all the mental activity I was involved in. I'm sure he thought I was a little crazy, but he challenged me to spell some words of his choosing alphabetically, and when I did, he wished me well in the use of my systems.

As for my American history class, the systems worked beautifully. On the first exam, my grade was 99; the closest grade to mine was 77. Four years later, I graduated Phi Beta Kappa—having put in something like one-fourth the study time that most students used.

Many years later, after I was traded to the New York Knickerbockers basketball team, I looked up Harry Lorayne. Our first meeting lasted over eighteen hours! Obviously, we had much in common, and we later became associated in our endeavors—including this book. It is, in fact, a combination of some of our ideas, thoughts on, systems of, memory.

Believe me, if you read about these systems and actually apply them as you go, there is no limit to how great your memory can be.

JERRY LUCAS

FOREWORD: HARRY LORAYNE

Unfortunately, I never had the opportunity to receive a formal education. I didn't complete the first year of high school. My grades, during that short time, were among the highest in my class. Why was this so? My IQ was average, and my "natural" memory was no better or worse than most people's. As a matter of fact, I originally was one of those many people who think they have the worst memory in the world.

I received good grades for one reason—I applied memory systems to my schoolwork. It's as simple as that.

Jerry has told you how he got hooked on alphabetizing words as a child. Well, as a very young boy *my* burning interest was card magic. I suppose I drove most of my friends up the wall, asking them to "pick a card, any card."

One of the "tricks" I performed during those years wasn't really a trick at all, it was a memory stunt. It consisted of memorizing an entire shuffled deck of playing cards, in order. All the cards were called off to me once, and I would know the position of every card in the deck! I still perform this stunt today, but at the time it was the only memory trick I knew.

One day, the thought struck—if I could apply a simple system to help me remember playing cards, why couldn't I do the same to help me remember anything I wanted to? That single simple thought started me on a lifetime career.

First I compiled a bibliography of all the material available on the subject of memory training. This started me thinking about and then devising my own systems. Years later, I started to perform for groups, organizations, conventions, and so on. My performance consisted of memory feats and demonstrations only. During these early years, literally thousands of people approached me after a performance to express their interest in learning "how to remember."

That is what led me to write my first book on the subject. It eventually sold over a million hardcover copies and was translated into nine languages.

Other books and courses on the art of a trained memory followed this first book. I have cartons full of the letters I received from people whose memories improved dramatically, thanks to my systems. One of these letters was from Jerry Lucas, then a freshman at Ohio State University.

We corresponded over the years. He had devised systems of his own, and his interest in the subject knew no bounds. He manipulated some of my systems, changed some of them to fit his purposes, applied them to his schoolwork. I could not have had a better or more dedicated disciple.

I went on with my work, Jerry went on with his. I eventually founded the Harry Lorayne School of Memory; Jerry became a championship basketball player. We still corresponded. A few years ago, Jerry started to demonstrate some of his mental abilities on national television. I had been doing the same thing for twenty years, including remembering the names and faces of up to five hundred people in the studio audience. Nobody, at that time, knew of any connection between Jerry and myself.

When Jerry was traded to the Knicks, we finally met. That first meeting, as Jerry has told you, lasted very nearly around the clock.

Even with our trained memories, Jerry and I would have been hard put to remember all the things we talked about. And so, at one point, we decided to run a tape recorder as we spoke. Throughout the book, you'll be reading small portions of that dialogue. Most, but not all, of these conversations were taken from that tape of our original meeting.

This will sound immodest, but it is my true feeling—I envy you! I envy you the discoveries you're about to make, the new areas you're about to explore, the pleasure of learning and enjoying at the same time. I wish I were in your place, right now.

HARRY LORAYNE

SOME HISTORY OF THE ART

Memory systems date back to antiquity. In the ancient world, a trained memory was of vital importance. There were no handy note-taking devices, and it was memory techniques and systems that enabled bards and storytellers to remember their stories, poems, and songs.

Early Greek and Roman orators delivered lengthy speeches with unfailing accuracy because they learned the speeches, thought for thought, by applying memory systems.

What they did, basically, was associate each thought of a speech to a part of their own homes. These were called "loci," or "places." The opening thought of a speech would, perhaps, be associated to the front door, the second thought to the foyer, the third to a piece of furniture in the foyer, and so on. When the orator wanted to remember his speech, thought for thought, he actually took a mental tour through his own home. Thinking of the front door reminded him of the first thought of his speech. The second "place," the foyer, reminded him of the next thought; and so on to the end of the speech. It is from this "place" or "loci" memory technique that we get the time-worn phrase "in the first place."

Although Simonides (circa 500 B.C.) is known as the father of the art of trained memory, scraps of parchment dating back a thousand years or so before Simonides state that memory techniques were an essential part of the orator's equipment.

Cicero wrote that the memories of the lawyers and orators of his time were aided by systems and training and in *De oratore* he described how he himself applied memory systems.

It's important to realize that oratory was an important career during those early days. "We should never have realized how great is the power [of a trained memory]," wrote the philosopher Quintilian, "nor how divine it is, but for the fact that it is memory which has brought oratory to its present position of glory."

The ancients also knew that memory training could help the thinking process itself. From a fragment dated about 400 B.C. we learn that "A great and beautiful invention is memory, always useful both for learning and for life." And Aristotle, after praising memory systems, said that "these habits too will make a man readier in reasoning."

If Simonides was the inventor of the art of trained memory, and Cicero its greatest early teacher, St. Thomas Aquinas was to become its patron saint, instrumental in making the art of trained memory a devotional and ethical art.

During the Middle Ages, monks and philosophers were virtually the only people who knew about and applied trained-memory techniques. The systems, whose use was mostly limited to religion, were basic to some religions. For example, memory systems were used to memorize Virtues and Vices, and some priests and philosophers taught that memory systems showed "how to reach Heaven and avoid Hell."

In 1491, Peter of Ravenna wrote *The Phoenix*, which became the best known of all early memory-training books and brought the art of trained memory out into the lay world. During the fifteenth and sixteenth centuries, many other books were written on the subject.

King Francis I of France used memory systems, as did England's Henry III. Shakespeare is held to have used trained-memory systems—his Globe Theater was called the "memory theater." Philosophers of the seventeenth century taught memory systems (Francis Bacon has one in his book *The Advancement of Learning*), and some scholars insist that Leibniz invented calculus while searching for a memory system that would aid in memorizing numbers.

So you see, there's nothing really new about trained-memory techniques. Unfortunately, the techniques fell into disuse for centuries. Some people who did practice them were actually regarded as witches. It's true that memory systems remained in use as a source of entertainment for others—in our own century, vaudeville players used memory systems to perform "mental tricks" onstage—but they were seldom if ever used for practical purposes or serious learning. Here and there someone would try to bring the systems to the fore again, but without success.

In a book titled *Memory*, William Stokes, a philosopher and memory teacher of the 1800's, summarizes the degree of public interest in the art of trained memory:

It is true . . . that notwithstanding the records of the past and the achievements, triumphs, and trophies of the present, the "educated," the intelligent masses—the world—know not and seem not to care to know its wondrous worth. The adoption of the science by a few paltry thousands cannot be regarded as anything when we consider the countless myriads peopling the earth—when we realize the fact that it is as essential to the proper exercise and full development of our intellectual existence as proper breathing is to our physical well-being; in spite of all that has been said and done, we may say comparatively—almost absolutely—that the art is a thing unknown!

There can be little doubt that before long, it will be generally recognized as an established science; and posterity will look back, and regard . . . this plea on behalf of memory . . . as an indication of the intellectual *darkness* of this age of boasted enlightenment. . . .

Let us hope that the day will come when it shall be considered as great a disgrace not to use memory systems as it is at present not to read!

Stokes's book was published in 1888. Nearly a century later, it is our pleasure to bring the art of trained memory back into the foreground—not only by teaching memory systems, but by bringing them to a level that the ancient (and not-so-ancient) thinkers would never have conceived as being within the realm of possibility.

2
IN THE FIRST PLACE:
ASSOCIATION

HL: Can't you picture those ancient orators, wandering around the streets of a city looking for other buildings to use as "places"?

JL: And the search made them more knowledgeable, not just better able to remember what they needed to. Eventually, they realized that any information that was already sequential could be used as loci or things to associate with *other* things.

HL: So when a searcher came across something like the signs of the zodiac, and realized that here he had twelve "places," he had to *learn* them first. And much later, some people realized that parts of the Bible could be used as places, so they had to learn that first.

JL: A case of knowledge begetting knowledge, wouldn't you say?

All memory, whether trained or untrained, is based on association. But that's stating it too simply. You will be taught many systems of association in this book, but it goes much deeper than that. You see, when people say, "I forgot," they didn't, usually—what really happened was that they didn't remember in the first place.

How can you forget something that you didn't *remember*, originally? Turn that around, and you have the solution to remembering—if you do remember something originally, how can you *forget* it?

That brings you to forcing yourself to remember originally.

How can you do this? The simple systems of association you'll learn here will do it *for* you, automatically!

One of the fundamentals of a trained memory is what we call Original Awareness. Anything of which you are Originally Aware *cannot* be forgotten. And, applying our systems of association will *force* Original Awareness. Observation is essential to Original Awareness—anything you wish to remember must first be observed. Using association will take care of that, too.

But how in the world do you associate something that's intangible or abstract? That question leads to another fundamental of trained memory. It is always easier to remember things that have meaning than it is to remember things that do not. You'll see, as you get a bit deeper into our methods, that *nothing* is abstract or intangible so far as the systems are concerned. You will learn how to make any intangible thing, any abstract piece of information, tangible and meaningful in your mind. Once you've mastered that simple technique, all remembering and therefore all learning will be easier for you for the rest of your life.

We'd like to insist right here that virtually all learning is based on memory. Educators don't like to admit it, but they know it's true. And any student knows that the more he remembers, the better grades he'll get from the teacher who likes to put down "memorization." We believe that there are three basic learning skills: 1) the search for information, 2) remembering the information, and 3) applying the information. The search is up to the educators and the sources of knowledge, the application is up to you. We'll take care of step 2.

Let's begin with association. First of all, you should realize that you've used association all your life. The problem is that you've usually associated subconsciously, without recognizing the association for what it was. Anything you clearly associated, even if subconsciously, is sure to have been easily remembered. But since you have no control over your subconscious, association has been a hit-or-miss kind of thing all your life.

Here's a basic memory rule: You Can Remember Any New Piece of Information if It Is Associated to Something You Already Know or Remember.

Do you remember the lines on the music staff, the treble clef, E, G, B, D, and F? If your teacher ever told you to think of the sentence Every Good Boy Does Fine, then you *do* remember them. Your teacher was following that basic memory rule, probably without realizing it. He or she was helping you to remember new (and abstract) information, the letters E, G, B, D, and F, by associating them to something you already knew, or at least understood—the simple sentence Every Good Boy Does Fine. Obviously, it worked.

Teachers in the early grades have been telling their students for years that it's easy to remember how to spell *piece* if you think of the phrase "a **pie**ce of **pie**." Since most young students already know how to spell *pie*, associating that old knowledge to the new—the spelling of "piece"—solves the problem. Again, the basic rule has been followed.

Very few people can easily remember the shape of Russia, or Greece, or any other country—except Italy, that is. That's because most people have been told, or have read, that Italy is shaped like a boot. There's that rule again—the shape of a boot was the something already known, and the shape of Italy *could not be forgotten* once that association was made.

These are common examples of association, subconscious or conscious. And so it goes: medical students use mnemonics (a technique for improving the memory) to help themselves remember the cranial nerves; other students picture **homes** on a **great lake** to help themselves remember that the five Great Lakes are **H**uron, **O**ntario, **M**ichigan, **E**rie, and **S**uperior; others picture a quartet being stabbed (**stab** gives you the initial letters of soprano, tenor, alto, and bass) to remember the four voices in a quartet. People have remembered that Mount Fujiyama is 12,365 feet high by associating it to a calendar (12 months, 365 days in a year).

The trouble with such examples is that they work only for those specific things; they're limited. The systems of trained memory you'll learn in this book are applicable to anything. They are limited only to the extent that your willingness to use them is limited. The point is this: If you know how to *consciously* associate anything you want to remember to something you already know, you'll have a trained memory. It's as simple as that. And you can learn to associate anything you like—quickly and naturally.

The trained-memory systems you'll be taught in this book are not unnatural in any way; they merely systematize, or pattern-ize, a natural process. Many times during your life you've heard or seen something that caused you to snap your fingers and say, "Oh, that reminds me. . . ." And, usually, the thing that reminded you of something had nothing to do with what it reminded you of. Somewhere back in your mind an absurd or random association had been made.

Why, when the orators of ancient times could use their own homes as "loci" to remind themselves of the thoughts of a speech, did they search for other buildings to give them more "places"? It wasn't that the same home or building couldn't be used over and over again—it could. ("The loci," said one thinker, "are like wax tablets which remain when what is written on them has been effaced and are ready to be written on again.")

No, the problem was that the "home" loci became too familiar after a while—after all, a staircase is a staircase, and a foyer is a foyer. But an important memory principle simply never occurred to the ancient orators: It isn't necessary to associate the thoughts of a speech, or anything else, to places—*the thoughts may be associated to each other,* so that one thought will remind you of the next thought.

That simple idea is the basis of the Link system of memory. First, we'll show you how to use it to help you memorize tangible items. Later on, when you've learned how to picture thoughts or concepts, you'll see that the idea can easily be applied to intangibles.

Right now, let's apply the basic association rule to remembering ten unrelated items. But we'll change the rule, slightly, by adding one important phrase. The revised rule: In Order to Remember Any New Piece of Information, It Must Be Associated to Something You Already Know or Remember *in Some Ridiculous Way.* The addition of that simple four-word phrase accomplishes quite a few things. It will force the Original Awareness that's necessary to remember anything, it will force you to concentrate and use your imagination as you never have before, and it will force you to form associations consciously.

Assume you wanted to memorize these ten items, in sequence: airplane, tree, envelope, earring, bucket, sing, basketball, salami, star, nose. All right, picture an **airplane** in your mind. There's no way to apply our memory rule yet. But now we come to the next item: tree.

The rule can now be applied, if we make the assumption that you already know, or remember, **airplane**. The new piece of information that you want to remember is **tree**. All you need to do is to form a ridiculous picture, or image, in your mind's eye—an association between those two things.

There are two steps involved. First you need a ridiculous —impossible, crazy, illogical, absurd—picture or image to associate the two items. What you don't want is a logical or sensible picture.

An example of a logical picture might be: an airplane parked near a tree. Though unlikely, that is not ridiculous, it is possible—therefore, it probably won't work. A ridiculous or impossible picture might be: A gigantic tree is flying instead of an airplane, or an airplane is growing instead of a tree, or airplanes are growing on trees, or millions of trees (as passengers) are boarding airplanes. These are crazy, impossible pictures. Now, select one of these pictures, or one you thought of yourself, and see it in your mind's eye.

We don't, of course, mean to see the words *airplane* and *tree.* You are to actually see the action you've selected—and most ridiculous associations between any two items will be actions, like the examples given here.

See that picture, that action, in your mind for a split second. You're not doing anything unusual; you've been seeing pictures in your mind all your life. Actually, you can't think without seeing pictures. Aristotle said it, centuries ago—one of his books opened with this sentence: "It is impossible even to think without a mental picture."

Seeing pictures, or images, in your mind is almost like having a movie screen in your head. If you read the words *husband, child, car,* etc., you cannot think of any of those people or things without "seeing" a picture of them—even if it's only for a split second. Try *not* to picture an elephant; *don't* see an elephant in your mind. What happened? It became impossible not to see, or picture, an elephant!

All right, then. Choose a ridiculous association between airplane and tree, and see it in your mind's eye, right now.

Once you've tried to do that, stop thinking about it. The "trying," however, is quite important. We tell our students that even if our systems don't work, they must work! That sounds silly, but it's true. Just trying to apply the systems must improve your memory, whether or not they really work. The fact that they do work, and work beautifully, will improve your memory to an unbelievable degree.

The next item on the list is **envelope.** We'll assume that you already know, or remember, tree. The new thing to remember is envelope. Simply form a ridiculous picture, or association, in your mind between tree and envelope. You might see millions of envelopes growing on a tree, or a tree is sealing a gigantic envelope, or you're trying to seal a tree in an envelope. There are many other suggestions we could give you, but all you need is *one* ridiculous picture. Select one of these, or one you thought of yourself, and see it in your mind's eye for an instant.

You needn't labor over seeing that picture. All it takes is a fraction of a second. It's the clarity of the picture that's important, not how long you see it. So see it, clearly, for just a second.

The next item to be remembered is **earring**. The thing you already know is envelope. Form a ridiculous association between envelope and earring. You might see yourself wearing envelopes instead of earrings, or you open an envelope and millions of earrings fly out and hit you in the face.

You're much better off, incidentally, thinking up your own pictures. When we suggest the ridiculous pictures, we're taking away some of your Original Awareness. We'll keep on giving you suggestions, but whether you use ours or your own, be sure to see the pictures *clearly*.

Select one of our associations between envelope and earring, or one you thought of yourself, and see it in your mind's eye.

Bucket is the new thing to remember. Associate it to earring. You might see yourself wearing buckets instead of earrings. Or, a gigantic bucket is wearing gigantic earrings. See one of these pictures in your mind.

The next thing to remember is **sing**. (This is not an object, not a noun, and it's here only to show you that this doesn't matter—an association will still remind you of it.) Associate sing to the last thing you already know—bucket. If you see a gigantic bucket singing, that will do it. Or you might see yourself singing with a bucket over your head. That's not impossible, but it's certainly ridiculous. Just be sure to see your picture clearly.

The next item is **basketball**. Associate that to sing. Picture a basketball singing. Or someone is singing and millions of basketballs fly out of his mouth.

Salami. Picture a gigantic salami playing basketball. Or a basketball player (Jerry Lucas, who else?) is dribbling a salami instead of a basketball.

Star. Picture a gigantic salami twinkling in the sky. Or you're slicing a star, instead of a salami! See the picture.

Nose. Picture someone with a twinkling star on his face instead of a nose. Or a star has a large nose. See that picture.

If you've tried to see all the pictures, you will know all ten items. The first item is the only one you may have trouble with, because you didn't associate it to anything to remind you of it. This will be straightened out for you soon enough. If you know the item, fine. If not, it was **airplane**. Try to think of the items before you read them in the paragraphs to follow. Now, think of airplane for a moment. What does that remind you of? **Tree**, of course.

Think of tree—that reminds you of . . . **envelope**. Think of envelope, which should remind you of . . . **earring**. Think of earring, and it will remind you of **bucket**. What silly thing was the bucket doing? Singing, of course—and that reminds you of **sing**. What else was singing? A **basketball**. Thinking of basketball for a moment will remind you of . . . **salami**. Salami should make you think of . . . **star**. And, finally, star will remind you of . . . **nose**.

How did you do? You should have known all of them. If you had trouble with one or two, if you think you forgot any, it's probably because you read the word here before you had the chance to think of it. You didn't "forget" it at all. If you're convinced that you did, then you didn't really remember it in the first place—go back to that item and *strengthen* your association. That is, be sure the picture is ridiculous, and, more important, be sure to really see it in your mind.

If you take paper and pencil and try it now, on your own, you'll see that you can list the ten items, in sequence, without missing any. Try it and see. Now, try it backward! Think of nose; that will make you think of . . . star. Star will remind you of . . . salami. That reminds you of . . . basketball. Basketball to . . . sing, sing to . . . bucket, bucket to . . . earring, earring to . . . envelope, envelope to . . . tree, and tree to . . . airplane. Try this with your own list, and you'll be proud of yourself—you'll be able to remember any list of items, in sequence, backward and forward.

3 THE LINK

HL: Of course, everyone knows that motivation is an important part of memory. The systems themselves can actually provide enough interest and challenge to add up to motivation.

JL: Without motivation, nobody would accomplish anything. When I was a senior in high school, I was named to the *Parade* magazine High School All-American Team. We were brought to New York City to be on the "Steve Allen Show" along with the All-American College Team, of which Wilt Chamberlain was a member. During the rehearsal, I was with Wilt in the lobby of the theater, where there was a high ledge—it must have been about twelve feet high. Someone approached Wilt and said, "Hey, Wilt, can you jump up and touch that ledge?"

Wilt said he thought he'd just forgotten how to jump. "But I'll tell you what," he said, "I'll bet you if you throw a hundred-dollar bill up there, I'd remember how to jump *real* quick!"

•

What you've learned in the preceding chapter is a tiny part of the Link system of memory. We call it the "Link" system because what you're doing when you apply it is linking one item to another, forming the links of a memory chain. One item *must* lead you to the next, if you're associating properly.

Having applied the Link system, you can retain any list for as long as you like. It's really hypothetical at the moment. When you start applying the Link for practical reasons, you're memorizing a list of things because you intend to *use* that list. It's the practical use that sets the retention—and provides the motivation to remember it in the first place. You'll see that this is so just as soon as you learn to apply it practically.

Although there's no reason why you should feel motivated to retain the list you memorized in the preceding chapter, you can if you want to. Simply go over it tomorrow; go over it mentally, that is, while you're driving or eating or whatever. Go over it again three days later, then go over it a week later, and you'll still know all the items in sequence. You'll know them for as long as you *want* to know them.

The Link system is used to remember things in sequence only, and there are many things that must be remembered, or learned, in sequence. A speech is a sequence of thoughts, a formula is a sequence of components, any number with more than two digits is a sequence. (You can't apply the Link system to numbers now because you don't yet know how to *picture* numbers. Later, you'll be using the Link to remember long-digit numbers.)

The one problem you may have in Linking, only at first, is in making your pictures ridiculous. There are four simple rules to help you do this right from the start. The easiest rule to apply is the rule of *Substitution*. That is, picture one item *instead of* the other. In the preceding chapter, we suggested that you might see a tree flying *instead of* an airplane. We were trying to force you to apply the rule of Substitution.

Another rule is *Out of Proportion*. Try to see the items larger than life. Check our suggestions again and you'll see that we used the word "gigantic" quite often. This was to force you to apply the rule of Out of Proportion.

Another rule is *Exaggeration*. Whenever the word "millions" was used, it was to force you to apply this rule. Try to see "millions" of an item.

And, try to get *Action* into your pictures. Action is always easy to remember. One suggestion was to see millions (exaggeration) of earrings flying out of an envelope and hitting you in the face. Hitting you was the action.

Applying one or more of these rules to any picture will help you to make that picture ridiculous. After a short while, you won't have to think about applying them; you'll do it automatically.

It does take some imagination to form ridiculous pictures in your mind. It's unfortunate that those "wheels" of imagination, observation, curiosity, enthusiasm, etc., that turned so quickly and smoothly when we were young have slowed down by the time we're adults. Society tends to do that, somehow. *Children* never have any problem forming silly or ridiculous pictures. They do it easily and naturally.

You'll find that our systems will start turning those wheels again; perhaps slowly at first, but turning nevertheless. Your imagination needs exercise, that's all. The important point is that simply *trying* to apply our systems will automatically give you that exercise. Your imagination must improve, as will your powers of observation, as you keep working with the systems. In a short while, you'll find that it will be the ridiculous, illogical picture that first comes to mind whenever you think of any two items.

Making the pictures ridiculous is what enables you to really see them; a logical picture is usually too vague. Once you really see the ridiculous picture, it does register in your mind. Research carried out by the department of basic and visual science at the Southern California College of Optometry indicates that when you actually see something, an electrical impulse reaches the vision center of the brain. They've also discovered (rediscovered scientifically, really, since ancient philosophers said the same thing) that there is not much physiological difference between the electrical signals that are activated *by the mind's eye* and ones that are activated *by the eye itself.*

So don't feel bad if, at first, you have to apply some effort in order to come up with those ridiculous pictures—at least, to come up with them quickly. That extra effort at first is good. It forces you to be Originally Aware.

We can't say it any better than it was said on parchment, in the scrolls called *Ad Herennium,* over three thousand years ago:

... Now nature herself teaches us what to do. When we see in everyday life things that are petty, ordinary, and banal, we generally fail to remember them, because the mind is not being stirred by anything novel or marvelous. But if we see or hear something exceptionally base, dishonorable, unusual, great, unbelievable, or ridiculous, that we are likely to remember for a long time. Accordingly, things immediate to our eye or ear we commonly forget; incidents of our childhood we often remember best. Nor could this be so for any other reason than that ordinary things easily slip from the memory while the striking and the novel stay longer in the mind.

Again, the idea, or the realization, is not new; it has just been neglected, or overlooked. Be sure, then, to make all your pictures ridiculous ones. In that way, and again from *Ad Herennium,* "Art will supplement nature." That's exactly what happens. When something assaults our senses in an unusual, great, unbelievable, or ridiculous way, it "stirs" the mind. It is usually retained without effort. It is the ordinary, everyday things that we have trouble remembering. Forming ridiculous pictures helps to make them outstanding, novel, or marvelous. The art (of trained memory) *is* supplementing nature, and all our systems are based on this fact.

If you can apply the Link and memorize ten items, then you can use it to remember twenty or thirty items. Of course, it will take more time to remember thirty items than it will to remember ten. But that would be so whether you applied the Link system or not. There is really no limit to the number of items you can memorize this way.

We strongly suggest that before you continue to the next chapter you try a Link on your own. Have someone give you fifteen or so items, and you form the Link. Or try it on your own. Make a list of items, and then Link them. After you've practiced awhile, when you feel fairly confident, show off for a friend.

Have him call off fifteen or sixteen items, as many as you feel comfortable with. Let him write them down as he calls them. If he doesn't, he won't be able to check you later because he won't remember the items himself (unless he's read this book). Also, his writing gives you the moment you need to make your association. For the time being, don't let him call off intangibles; he's to choose concrete things, nouns or active verbs.

When he's called the fifteen or sixteen items, you call them right back to him, by memory. If you miss one or two, there's no problem. Simply ask him what they are, strengthen that particular association, and then call off the items backward!

And how will you be sure to remember the first item called? Well, once you start using the Link for practical purposes, that won't be a problem. The subject you're memorizing will *start* your Link.

But even for now the problem is really a hypothetical one. If you think of any item near the start of your Link and work backward, you must eventually come to the first item. And, to save you even this small amount of time: When your friend calls the first item, just associate it—to *him*.

Take the list in the preceding chapter. If your friend called "airplane" as the first item, you might look at him and see an airplane on his head. That's all it takes. The next item is associated to airplane, and so on to the end of the Link.

When you're ready to call off the list of items, simply look at your friend. You'll "see" the airplane on his head, and that association will lead you through the rest of the list.

Again, we suggest that you try a few test Links before continuing. Show off for your friends, or make your own list and show off to yourself. We suggest showing off only because we know that each time you do, you'll gain confidence. You'll see that the system works!

4 *SUBSTITUTE WORDS*

HL: I've never met anyone who hasn't at times come up with a similar-sounding word or phrase when thinking of something completely different—like "can't elope" and "cantaloupe."

JL: I know one example that was even used in a song—"chicken in a car, and the car can't go—that's how you spell 'Chicago'!"

HL: My favorite is children saying the Lord's Prayer who don't understand the word "temptation." In the New York area, the phrase is likely to come out: "Lead us not into *Penn Station!*"

•

The states of the United States can easily be memorized in alphabetical sequence. Of course, you probably couldn't care less about knowing the states in sequence. That's not the point. The point is to show you how to picture abstractions, like names. Again, once you understand how to make an intangible tangible and meaningful, it becomes easy to remember. This will be a good exercise for the Link, and it will also start you on the Substitute Word system of memory.

The Substitute Word concept can be applied to any seemingly abstract material. Basically, it's this: When you hear or see a word or phrase that seems abstract or intangible to you, think of something—anything—that sounds like, or reminds you of, the abstract material and *can be pictured* in your mind.

Ordinarily, the name of a person, thing, or place cannot be pictured in the mind. Most names are intangible, which is why they're so difficult to remember. For example, there would seem to be no way to "picture" (or associate) Minnesota. You might, however, easily picture a **mini soda**, a small bottle of soda. Mini soda sounds like Minnesota, and must remind you of it. And you can associate mini soda to anything you like. If you were trying to memorize the states in their alphabetical order, you might associate mini soda to **Mrs. sip**; perhaps a married lady is sipping a little soda. This would remind you that Mississippi follows Minnesota, alphabetically.

Ordinarily, you could not "picture" Maryland and Massachusetts. But you could picture a girl named **Mary** (or a bride, **marry**) **land**ing among a **mass** of people who **chew** and **sit**. Marry land must remind you of Maryland, and mass chew sit will certainly remind you of Massachusetts. Now, you may be wondering how you'd know which of the two items in your picture comes first. Well, aside from the fact that they're alphabetical in this particular example, which comes first is a problem only because we're discussing two at a time. When you actually Link all of them, or more than two, it's no problem. That's the whole point of the Link; one item must lead you to the next.

To repeat, you do have to use a bit of imagination, and the more often you form conscious associations, the easier it will become because you will be improving your imagination as you improve your memory. As Aristotle explained in *De anima*,

The perceptions brought in by the five senses are first treated or worked upon by the faculty of imagination, and it is the images so formed which become the material of the intellectual faculty. Imagination is the intermediary between perception and thought.

It is the image-making part of the mind which makes the work of the higher processes of thought possible. Hence the mind never thinks without a mental picture. The thinking faculty thinks of its forms in pictures. No one could ever learn or understand anything, if he had not the faculty of perception; even when he thinks speculatively, he must have some mental picture with which to think.

Aristotle went on to say that all men can think because "it is possible to put things before our eyes, the way those who invent trained-memory techniques teach us to construct images."

We are teaching you, now, how to "construct images" with intangibles. The pictures (Substitute Words, thoughts, or phrases) that you use must remind you of the intangible material. And, again, simply *trying* to apply the idea must better your memory. Trying to find a Substitute Word for anything *forces* you to think about it, to concentrate on it as you normally would not.

If, during any of the examples in this book, the Substitute Word does not remind you of what you wanted to remember, it's undoubtedly because you used *our* suggestion for the Substitute Word, which didn't work for you. Usually, it will—but you're certainly better off thinking up your own Substitute Words, thoughts, or phrases. Again, our giving you suggestions does remove the necessity for you to use your own imagination, thereby diminishing your Original Awareness.

Still, we have no choice but to give you suggestions for most of the examples we'll be using. If you want to use those suggestions, fine. But be sure to form good, clear pictures in your mind.

Getting back to the states, do you see now that if you make up a Substitute Word or phrase for each state and then Link them, you can memorize them all? It's easy to do, and it's fun.

If you don't want to memorize them all in sequence, try it with some of them—just for the practice and the (imagination) exercise. Linking all of them would be excellent practice for forming Substitute Words or phrases, and forming pictures and associations for your Link.

Here are all the states, listed alphabetically and numbered

from 1 to 50. Later, after learning the Peg system, you can turn back to this page and try memorizing them by number. As you Link them, pause after every ten or so to review mentally the pictures you've formed up to that time.

1. Alabama	14. Indiana	27. Nebraska	40. South Carolina
2. Alaska	15. Iowa	28. Nevada	41. South Dakota
3. Arizona	16. Kansas	29. New Hampshire	42. Tennessee
4. Arkansas	17. Kentucky	30. New Jersey	43. Texas
5. California	18. Louisiana	31. New Mexico	44. Utah
6. Colorado	19. Maine	32. New York	45. Vermont
7. Connecticut	20. Maryland	33. North Carolina	46. Virginia
8. Delaware	21. Massachusetts	34. North Dakota	47. Washington
9. Florida	22. Michigan	35. Ohio	48. West Virginia
10. Georgia	23. Minnesota	36. Oklahoma	49. Wisconsin
11. Hawaii	24. Mississippi	37. Oregon	50. Wyoming
12. Idaho	25. Missouri	38. Pennsylvania	
13. Illinois	26. Montana	39. Rhode Island	

Trying to memorize these from the top, you start by thinking up a Substitute Word that reminds you of Alabama. **Album** will do nicely. An album can be pictured, whereas Alabama cannot. If you're old enough to remember a song called "I'm Alabamy Bound," which had to do with a train, you might have thought of that and pictured a train. For Alaska, you can picture the flaming dessert **baked Alaska**, or **I'll ask her**, or **a last car**. Now start your Link: You might picture a gigantic album serving baked Alaska to other albums.

For Arizona, you can use **air zone** as the Substitute phrase. Picture a gigantic piece of baked Alaska floating in the air, over a safety zone. For Arkansas, you might see yourself sawing an ark; associate that picture to air zone.

Please bear in mind that *anything* can be pictured, a noun, an action, whatever. Remember, *sing* was used in the first sample

Link—and you could, and did, picture *sing* as well as any of the other items, which were all nouns.

For Arizona and Arkansas, an **ark and** a **saw** floating in the **air** over a safety **zone** would do the trick. For California, how about **call a fawn** as a Substitute Word? To associate that to Arkansas, you could picture yourself calling a fawn into an ark. Whatever Substitute phrase you use, be sure to really see the pictures.

California to Colorado (**color a toe**). You might see that fawn painting (coloring) one of his toes.

Colorado to Connecticut (**connect a cut**). You cut the colored toe, then connect the two parts.

Connecticut to Delaware (**Della wear**). A girl named Della is wearing flowing robes as she bends over to connect a cut.

Delaware to Florida (**flower there**). Della throws those flowing robes to the floor and a gigantic flower grows there.

Florida to Georgia (**George**). The gigantic flower is named ... George! Or, millions of flowers are growing in a **gorge**.

If you've made these or your own associations and have seen the pictures in your mind, you know the first ten states just as you knew the ten items in the first sample Link. There are, of course, many other Substitute Words you could have used. If you thought of the Everglades when you thought of Florida, picturing its swamps would have served the purpose for you. Remember that Linking is individual, personal—what you think of is usually best for you. And, most often, the first Substitute Word that comes to mind is the best to use.

If you want to practice some more, review the first ten states in sequence and then continue your Link with the next ten. Perhaps, George to **how are ya**; how are ya to **Ida hoe** or **potato**; potato to **ill noise**; ill noise to **Indian**; to **I owe her**; to **can sass**; to **can't talk**; to **lose Anna**; to water **main** (pipe); to **marry land**. We'll leave the associations here up to you.

Review the Link, the twenty states, then continue with the

next ten, and so on. If you can provide your own Substitute Words for the remaining states, without using the suggestions that follow, all the better.

Michigan, **mix again**; Missouri, **misery**; Montana, **mountain**; Nebraska, **new brass car**; Nevada, **never there**, gambling; New Hampshire, **hamster**; New Jersey, **Jersey** cow; New Mexico, **Mexican** sombrero; New York, **new cork**, Empire State Building; North Carolina, **carry liner**. (Make up a "standard" for *north* and *south* and use them all the time. For example, you might use **snow** to represent north, and **mouth** to represent south. A picture of someone carrying a liner [ship] in a snowstorm would therefore remind you of North Carolina.)

To continue Substitute Words: North Dakota, **decoder**; Ohio, **oh, hi!, higher!**; Oklahoma, **homer**; Oregon, **are gone**; Pennsylvania, **pencil**; Rhode Island, **rode**; South Carolina, **carry liner** (perhaps carrying a liner in your **mouth**); South Dakota, **decoder**; Tennessee, **tennis (see)**; Texas, **taxes**; Utah, **you tear**; Vermont, **vermin**; Virginia, **virgin**; Washington, **wash**; West Virginia, **best virgin**; Wisconsin, **wise cousin**; Wyoming, **roaming**.

If you've gone down the list of states ten at a time, using the combination of Substitute Words and Linking, then reviewing each ten once learned, you should be able to reel off all fifty states with hardly a stumble.

Try it—and if you miss a few, simply go back and strengthen those particular associations. You'll be surprised at how easy it is to remember something most people would find difficult, if not impossible.

5 LONG WORDS, APPOINTMENTS AND ERRANDS, SHOPPING LISTS

JL: So, Simonides, who was attending a large banquet, was called out to receive a message, and the building collapsed. All the diners were killed. Simonides was able to identify every mangled body for burial purposes. When he was asked how he'd done it, he said that he'd used a memory system.

HL: The banquet may have been large, but Lucius Scipio was supposedly able to remember the names and faces of all the citizens of ancient Rome.

JL: I'll bet you've met and remembered more people than that in your career, Harry.

HL: That's true—at the last count I'd met and remembered somewhere around twenty million people. I can start my own country!

JL: During his news conferences, General George Marshall used to listen to reporters' questions without breaking the continuity of his prepared statement. When he finished the statement, he'd look at each reporter and answer his question in turn. What he did was, he associated the key word or thought of the question to the reporter's name or face. And James Farley's fantastic memory for names and faces supposedly helped elect Franklin D. Roosevelt to his first term.

HL: Did you know I met David Roth? And his fame as a memory expert goes back to the early 1900's. The last time I spoke to him, he told me that his local Rotary Club was giving a luncheon in honor of his ninety-sixth birthday. He told me, "I won't do much, Harry—I'm just going to remember everybody's telephone number." And there were two hundred people there!

JL: So maybe people with trained memories live longer. Using trained-memory systems certainly does keep a person more alert and aware. Which might have something to do with longevity.

HL: Let's hope so!

•

The famous chess player Harry Pillsbury was almost as well known for his memory as for his skill at chess. He was once challenged by two professors to memorize up to thirty words or phrases, read to him only once. Pillsbury repeated them in correct sequence, and then in reverse order. He also knew them the following day. This garnered quite a bit of publicity for Pillsbury, yet the feat is fairly easy to accomplish—if you apply the Link and the Substitute Word systems of memory.

Now, the words and phrases that were read to Pillsbury were not quite so easy to grasp as a list of everyday items or the states of the union. They were: antiphlogistine, periosteum, takadiastase, plasmon, threlkeld, streptococcus, staphylococcus, micrococcus, plasmodium, Mississippi, freiheit, Philadelphia, Cincinnati, athletics, no war, Etchenberg, American, Russian, philosophy, Piet Potgelter's Rost, salmagundi, oomisillecootsi, Schlechter's Nek, Manyinzama, theosophy, catechism, Madjescomalops.

You can remember them all, in sequence, by applying the two systems you've already learned—the Link and the Substitute

Word. **Auntie flog a stein** would remind you of antiphlogistine. Associate that silly picture to, perhaps, **pear eat a steam** (periosteum). You might see your auntie (or any little old lady—whatever auntie conjures up in your mind) flogging a (beer) stein as she eats a gigantic pear that's steaming hot. Try to see that picture.

Pear eat a steam to, perhaps, **tack a dais daze**. A gigantic pear that's eating a steam (radiator) is tacking up a dais (platform); the pear is in a daze as he does it. For the next association you might see a **plastic man** (plasmon) tacking up a dais.

Now, plastic man to **thrill cold** (threlkeld), to **strap to cock** (rooster) and **ass** (donkey), to **staff ill of carcass**, to **micro cock ass**, to **place my dime**, to **Mrs. sip**, to **fry height**, to **fill a dell for ya** (or **Philadelphia** brand cream cheese), to **sin sin at tea**, to people performing **athletics**, to **no war**, to **etchin'** (ice)berg, to **a merry can**, to **Russian** roulette, to **fill a sofa**, to **pie et** (ate) **pot** (of) **gal tears rust**, to **sell my gun D**, to **ooh, my silly coat see**, to sh, **let us neck**, to **many in summer**, to **tea owes a fee**, to **cat kiss 'im**, to **Madge's comb elopes**.

This may seem like a lot of work to you. Well, it will certainly take more time and effort than, say, remembering twenty-seven simple items. But just think of how much work it would be to memorize twenty-seven words like this *without* a system. Not only would that require an enormous amount of time and effort, but you'd probably never accomplish it. Forming Substitute Words, phrases, or thoughts, and Linking, on the other hand, is fun; it *forces* you to use your imagination and to concentrate; and above all—it works!

Whatever any Substitute phrase conjures up in your mind is what you should use for the picture. For **sell my gun D**, you might see yourself selling your gun to a gigantic letter D. (In another chapter, you'll learn how letters of the alphabet can themselves be pictured, concretely and easily.) You might have thought of **sailor my gun die**—a sailor takes your (my) gun and kills himself with it. Whatever you think of and see will work for you.

Take a few moments to see if you can remember all the words listed above. If Pillsbury could do it, so can you! You may be surprised at the facility with which you can do it.

Linking difficult words is like swinging two bats to help you swing one better. It isn't often necessary to remember words like that. But the idea of the Link can, of course, be wonderfully practical. Later on, we'll show you how to remember specific weekly appointments, by day and hour. For now, if you need to remember simple errands and appointments during most normal days, you can use a simple Link; usually no Substitute Words are necessary.

Assume it is important that you remember to pick up a lamp you ordered. You also must remember to buy a package of typing paper. Start a Link; associate lamp to paper. Perhaps you see yourself putting a lighted lamp, instead of paper, into your typewriter. Or a gigantic sheet of paper is on your bedside table, you pull a string—and it lights like a lamp. Select one of these pictures, or one you thought of yourself, and see it in your mind.

You don't want to forget to pick up your suit at the cleaners. Continue the Link: perhaps you're wearing sheets of typing paper instead of a suit.

You promised to call about arranging for swimming lessons for your child. See a suit, with nobody in it, swimming or diving into a pool.

For days, you've been meaning to buy some lightbulbs. Picture gigantic lightbulbs swimming.

You must remember to visit a friend at the hospital. Picture yourself putting your friend, instead of a lightbulb, into a socket.

You want to pick up a roll of stamps before the post office closes. Picture your sick friend lying on (and sticking to) a gigantic stamp instead of a hospital bed. Or you're licking your friend and sticking him on an envelope.

If you've actually visualized the silly pictures, you'll remember the things you must do. Start with **lamp**—that should remind you of the next chore or errand, and so on. When applying this idea practically, you'd form your Link the night before. Then, in the morning, you'd simply go over that Link while getting dressed or having breakfast.

If you think of something else you want to accomplish that day, tack it on to the end of your Link. It's important to go over your Link before you leave, because thinking of the chores will remind you to take whatever you need from your home in order to accomplish the errand. For example, if you need a receipt in order to get your suit from the cleaners, thinking of the suit will remind you to go to your desk and get the receipt.

During the day, go over your Link every once in a while—or while you're walking, eating, whatever. Anytime you think of an errand that you have not yet done, you'll know it; simply go and do it. As a final check, go over the Link before you prepare to go home.

This practical use of the Link will save you plenty of time and aggravation. The worst that can happen is that it won't work completely and you'll forget an errand. Well, you haven't much to lose—you've been doing *that* all your life!

Exactly the same idea can be applied to remembering a shopping list. Granted, remembering a shopping list is not the most important thing in the world. But people who make out a shopping list on a piece of paper often either forget to take it with them, or forget to look at it until they get home again.

Simply Link the items you want to purchase. Be sure to make the pictures ridiculous—you're peeling an **orange** and there's a container of **milk** (or a cow) inside it; you're milking a cow and slices of **bread**, instead of milk, come out, etc. Once inside the supermarket, just go over your Link every once in a while. If you do this, you won't forget *any* items.

6 SPEECHES

JL: After I graduated from Ohio State, I was booked to speak at a high school athletic banquet. I got plenty of applause, but just as everyone was leaving, this kid comes up to me and says, "Mr. Lucas, I enjoy watching you play basketball—but I thought that was the worst speech I ever heard in my life!"

Well, his mother was right behind him, and of course she heard. "Oh, Mr. Lucas," she said, "please pay no attention to him. He only repeats what he hears!"

HL: I got zinged by a "repeater" *before* a speech, once. I always tell the chairman of the group how to introduce me. To save time, I make it short and simple, and I always say it in exactly the same way. This particular time, when I was the after-dinner speaker, I told the chairman to say, "Ladies and gentlemen, we have a surprise for you this evening, something different, unique, blah, blah, blah. You've seen him on TV, et cetera, et cetera." He took notes as I spoke.

We finished our meal, and the chairman went to the lectern to introduce me. He said, "Ladies and gentlemen, we have a surprise for you this evening, something different, unique, *blah . . . blah . . . blah*. You've seen him on . . ."!

•

Probably the worst mistake you can make is to try to memorize a speech word for word. First of all, it isn't really necessary. The assumption is that if you've been asked to deliver a speech on a particular subject, you *know* something about that subject.

Secondly, memorizing the speech word for word will make it sound that way when you deliver it—memorized. And, finally, when you memorize a speech word for word, you're taking the chance of fumbling over one word you can't remember. Why take that chance when there are probably dozens of other words that would do?

Reading a speech doesn't work either, because you want to hold the group's attention, and reading to them is likely to put them to sleep. Even if you occasionally look up at your audience as you read, it won't help much. As a matter of fact, that's the moment when you're likely to lose your place and start hemming and hawing as you try to find it.

The best way to deliver a speech is to talk it in your own words, *thought for thought*. A speech is a *sequence* of thoughts; if the thoughts are out of sequence, the speech won't make much sense. Now, you know how to use the Link system to remember things in sequence. The Link, plus one other idea, will help you to remember your speech thought for thought.

First, write out or type your speech, including all the things you want to say about all the ideas you think are important. Read it over to get the gist of it. Now for that "other idea": Select a Key Word from each thought that will *remind you of the entire thought.*

This is easier to do than it might seem. There is rarely a thought, whether it is to be expressed in one sentence or two paragraphs, that cannot be brought to mind by *one* word or phrase. It is these Key Words (or Key Thoughts) that you Link —at which point you have the speech memorized thought for thought!

Here are some excerpts from a talk delivered at a convention to a group of merchants and dealers selling the same line of products. The speaker was asked to talk about a sharp drop in profits over the previous two years and to suggest ways of doing something about it.

The talk originally took thirty-five minutes to deliver. Excerpts have been culled from it to demonstrate the Key Words or Thoughts that the speaker wanted to get across.

The problem is an obvious one. We're all selling just as many of the product as we always have, but our *profit margin* has been drastically reduced. The reasons, too, are obvious. The cost of material and manufacture has gone up, and so have our prices. The trouble is that if we raise our prices any higher, we'll lose sales. What we have to do is find ways to raise our profit margin. . . .

We have to get more people to *walk in* to our stores. Obviously, the more people that walk in to our stores, the more opportunities we have to make sales. Perhaps we can organize contests, etc. . . .

An important part of each of our businesses depends on building a *good name* in each of our local areas. There are many ways to do this; relaxing our "no return" policy. . . .

Our products are *nationally advertised,* but we haven't been taking advantage of that at all. At least, not to my knowledge. We've got to plan local advertising to mesh with national advertising; blowups of the national ads in our windows should be considered, and. . . .

The *new line,* Starbright, Holly, Baby Soft, Meteor, and Honeymoon, is really good, and should help to stir up some fresh business. It's been a long time since we had any new line of product at all. . . .

We also must work harder to turn *bread and butter* sales. Why should a customer walk out after buying only the item she came for? A little thought, and effort, would help toward finding ways to almost force the customer to buy at least one other item, perhaps just an accessory, to go with the one she bought. A two-for-one sale might work, or. . . .

And how can we make customers *come back* to the store? How

many of you follow up a sale? How many of you take advantage of the names and addresses on your sales receipts that are gathering dust in your files? Use those names—send notes and notices of sales. . . .

The Key Words have been italicized within each of the thoughts of this talk. Let us emphasize that the speaker knew what he wanted to say about each thought—that wasn't his problem. What he wanted to avoid was omitting an entire thought. Forming a Link takes care of that.

There are two ways to do this. You can either list or underline the Key Words, and then Link them; or you can Link them as you go. As you become more proficient, you'll most likely Link the Key Words as you go.

Now. The first Key Word or Thought is **profit margin**. Use a Substitute Word to remind you of it. Perhaps your **Ma** is drinking **gin** and being paid for it—she's making a **profit**. That will certainly remind you of the thought; if you were delivering this talk, either **Ma gin** or **profit** alone would suffice.

The next Key Word is **walk in**. Associate **Ma gin** and/or **profit** to that; a silly picture of your gin-drinking Ma **walking in** to a store will do it. The next Key Word is **good name**. Continue the Link; you might see a **name** (picture gigantic letters of your name, or a gigantic business card) that's **good**, walking into a store.

Good name to **nationally advertised**. You might see your good name being on the cover of a **national magazine**.

Nationally advertised to **new line**. See a ridiculous picture of a long **line** of national magazines hot off the press—they're **new**.

New line to **bread and butter**. See a long line of **bread and butter**.

Bread and butter to **come back**. Picture yourself calling a gigantic piece of bread and butter to **come back**.

Forming such a Link accomplishes two things. It forces you to concentrate on (to be Originally Aware of) the thoughts of the speech, and it will give you the sequence of thoughts. *Knowing* that you definitely have that sequence also gives you a confidence that you wouldn't otherwise have.

Thinking of the first thought, **Ma gin**, is all you need to remind you that you want to talk about the reduction of the profit margin—so talk about it, say it in your own words. When you've said all you have to say about that, you'll automatically be reminded of **walk in**. Since you wrote the speech, you'll know just what **walk in** refers to; it will remind you of the entire thought. Just say what you want to say about getting people to walk in to the store.

If you made the ridiculous association, the Key Word **walk in** must remind you of **good name**. Talk about that; then **good name** will remind you of **nationally advertised**, at which point you say what you have to say about that thought. And so on, to the end of your speech.

You need only try this idea to see that it will work for you. You might be wondering what you'd do if you had a few facts to remember that pertained to a particular thought. For example, take the product names listed within the **new line** thought—you simply form an "offshoot" or "tangent" Link. That is, after you've formed your basic Link, go back to **new line** and form an offshoot Link of the names.

You might see a picture of a long **line** of **bright stars**; bright stars are forming a **holly** wreath on your door; you're holding a holly wreath in your arms like a **baby**—it's very **soft**; a baby is shooting across the sky like a **meteor**; two meteors are going on a **honeymoon**.

You'll see, when you're delivering the speech, that **new line** will lead you right through the offshoot Link, reminding you of the product names. Then, you'll still be reminded of the thought you originally associated to **new line** in the basic Link—**bread and butter**. If the products have style numbers, you can Link them, too—once you've learned how to picture numbers.

If, for some reason, you want to remember the speech virtually word for word, you'll find that simply going over it a few more times will do the trick. Since you wrote the speech yourself, your own words would be the most likely ones to come to mind as you voiced each thought.

This same system—a combination of the Link and the Key Thought ideas—can be applied to reading material or lectures in almost exactly the same way. Simply Link Key Words as you read or listen. Applied to reading material, the idea forces you to read actively, with concentration; applied to lectures, it does the same thing. It's difficult to allow your mind to wander when you're listening for Key Words to remind you of thoughts. The next time you want to remember more of reading or lecture material than you usually do, try applying what you've learned here. You'll be surprised at how much you retain.

The system can also be applied to song lyrics and scripts. Apply the same idea, then go over the material a few more times. It's still necessary to remember the material thought for thought first; *then* you worry about word for word. The language itself is a memory aid—there are certain ways to say certain things. Once you definitely know the sequence of thoughts, the words tend to take care of themselves. If you know the thought, the worst that can happen is that you'll say the line a bit differently from the way it was written; it's when you don't know the thought that you can really "go up" (have no idea what comes next).

One famous, award-winning actress has for some time applied these ideas to all her difficult-to-memorize scripts. In a letter, she wrote that the systems "make what is a usual drudgery part of the creative art!"

We'll be giving you more help in remembering reading material later on in the book. For now, you might want to apply the same basic idea to help you remember jokes and anecdotes. Two memory problems may have to be solved: remembering the joke in the first place, and remembering the idea of the joke, its premise and punchline.

To remember jokes, many professional comedians Link a Key Word or thought of one joke to the Key Word of the next, and so on. The comedian knows the jokes; he simply needs reminders of the jokes and their sequence. So, a Link of orange to politics to elephant to gas pump would be enough to remind a comedian to tell the joke about oranges, then the one about politics, and so on.

Remembering the idea and punchline of a joke is just as easy. Let's remember this old gag:

"How do you make a Venetian blind?"

"Stick a finger in his eye!"

Simply form a silly association. Picture a venetian blind with one large eye on your window—see a gigantic finger going into that eye. That's all. You'll remember the idea and the punchline of the joke.

7 FOREIGN AND ENGLISH VOCABULARY

JL: When I played on the United States basketball team during the 1960 Olympics in Rome, our first game was to be against the Japanese team. I asked one of the interpreters to teach me a couple of Japanese phrases, so I'd be able to say something to the Japanese players the next morning.

I had no trouble with the phrase "good morning," because it's pronounced *ohio* in Japanese, and of course I associated it to my home state. I easily learned a few more phrases by applying the systems.

The game was scheduled for 9:30 A.M. Just before it was about to start, I looked over at my opponent and said, "Ohio, gozai mosk," which means, "Good morning, how are you?" He gave me a big smile, happy to have found somebody from America who could speak his language.

Well, he backed out of the jump circle and began to bow to me, rattling off Japanese as fast as he could. This created quite a scene, because he was so engrossed in this conversation he thought he was going to carry on with me that he forgot he was there to play a basketball game.

One referee was from Russia, the other from France, and I spoke only English. The Japanese player and the officials each spoke only their own languages. So there were the four of us trying to talk to each other—nobody knowing what the other was saying. They had to call time out, we had to go back to the sidelines, and we had to start the game later. Then the player rattled Japanese at me throughout the entire game. Of course I didn't know the Japanese words to tell him I didn't know Japanese, so I must have said "Good morning" to him dozens of times during that game! He couldn't have been more pleased.

HL: Had you had the time to apply the systems to Japanese for a week before that game, you'd have had plenty of things besides "ohio" to say to him.

JL: Sure, but then he'd have gotten so excited it might have thrown his game off!

•

Now that you've learned how to apply the Substitute Word idea to intangible words and names—and Link them—you can go a step further. Instead of associating, say, one state to the next in order to form a Link, you can associate a state to its capital city. You can also associate a word to its meaning, whether it's an English word or a foreign word.

This brings us to an important point. Most often, where memory is concerned, an entity consists of two things. Even the most complicated-seeming memory chores can usually be broken down into entities of two: a name to a face, an address to a person or company, a price or style number to an item, a telephone number to a person or company, a definition or meaning to a word, and so on. Even when forming a long Link, you're still basically working with only two items at a time.

The capital city of Maryland is Annapolis (that's right; it is not Baltimore); if you form a ridiculous association of a bride (**marry**) **land**ing on **an apple**, you'll find it difficult to forget. The capital of Wyoming is Cheyenne; you might picture a **shy** girl, named **Ann**, carrying a large letter **Y** and **roaming**. Michigan's capital is Lansing; associate **mix again** to **land sing**. California's is Sacramento; associate **call a fawn** to **sack cement toe**. Tennessee's is Nashville; associate **tennis** to **gnash**ing your teeth (see a tennis racket gnashing its teeth). Vermont's is Montpelier; associate **vermin** to **mount peeler**. Apply this to any state whose capital you'd like to remember, and whenever you think of the state, the capital city will surely come to mind.

The same system can be applied to Presidents and Vice-Presidents. Associate the Substitute Word for the name of the one to the Substitute Word for the name of the other. For example, President Rutherford B. Hayes's Vice-President was named Wheeler. Associate **hay** to **wheel** in order to remember that. If you picture the hay saying, **"oh, hi,"** to the wheel, you'll also be reminded of the fact that Hayes was from Ohio.

JL: I've applied the systems to Japanese, Polish, Russian, and a few other languages, but never to Portuguese—for the simple reason that I've never been to Portugal.

HL: I spent most of one summer there, and I knew even before I got there that Portuguese is a difficult language to learn. Anyway, they have terrific clams in Portugal, and I love clams. In the very first restaurant I visited, I found out that the Portuguese word for clams is *amejues,* pronounced *ah-mezz-you-iz.* I immediately saw a picture of a gigantic clam approaching me, all drippy and dirty, and I say to it, "What a mess you is!" So before I learned how to say, "Do you have," when the waiter approached I just said "amejues" and got them.

JL: Which is all you were interested in at the moment.

HL: Exactly. People who need a doctor in a foreign country don't have to be able to say "Please call a" or "Take me to a." But they'd better know the word for doctor!

The Substitute Word idea can be applied to any word of any

language. There is no word that does not sound like, or make you think of, something in your own language. To remember the meaning of a simple French word like *père* (father), you might picture a gigantic **pear** being your father. For *pont* (bridge), you might see yourself **punt**ing a bridge instead of a football.

The idea applies to any word, short or long. The French word for grapefruit is *pamplemousse*. Picture huge yellow **pimples** all over a **moose**; each pimple is actually a grapefruit. If you try to see any of these silly pictures, the system must work—for reasons you already know: You're forcing yourself to be Originally Aware, you're really concentrating on the word, and you're forcing yourself to use your imagination. There just is no way to apply the Substitute Word system to a foreign word *without* concentrating on or being Originally Aware of that word, and using some imagination. And finally, applying the system reminds you of the two things (that entity of two mentioned before) you must know: the pronunciation of the foreign word, and its English equivalent.

If you used our or your own Substitute Word and saw a ridiculous picture, the next time you hear or see *pamplemousse*, it must make you think of a moose with grapefruit pimples. When you hear, see, or think *grapefruit*, the same thing will happen. Students of ours do this with twenty foreign words in an evening, every evening, and remember them all easily—simply because the intangible, abstract conglomeration of sounds of the foreign word is changed to a definite, tangible picture in the mind.

Since Portuguese has been mentioned, let's use a few Portuguese words as examples. *Walnut* in Portuguese is *noz*, pronounced *nawsh*. Simply picture a gigantic walnut being **nauseous**, or you eat a gigantic walnut and it makes you **nauseous.** See that picture. The word for a woman's *skirt* is *saia*, pronounced *syer*. Picture a skirt sighing—it's a **sigher.** A *peach* is a *pêssego,* pronounced *pess-a-goo.* See a gigantic peach asking you to **pass the goo.**

A woman's *purse* is a *bolsa.* Picture a gigantic purse made of **balsa** wood, or a large piece of **balsa** wood carrying a purse.

The word for *dinner* is *jantar,* pronounced *John-tar* (the *n* is really a nasal sound). Picture **John** eating **tar** for dinner.

Handkerchief is *lenço,* pronounced *leng-ssoo* (the *ng* is a nasal sound). Picture yourself **lend**ing **Sue** your handkerchief; make the picture ridiculous; perhaps you're lending her millions of handkerchiefs or one gigantic one.

Father is *pai,* pronounced *pie.* A gigantic **pie** is your father.

A *strawberry* is a *morango,* pronounced *moo-ran-goo.* See a gigantic strawberry, or millions of them, eating **meringue goo.**

The word for *socks* is *peúgas,* pronounced *pee-oo-gesh.* You might picture a gigantic sock that has a terrible odor; you say, "**Peeyoo,** it smells like **gas.**"

Bear in mind that if you were trying to really learn a particular language, you'd be aware of the basic sounds and letters. In the last example, "true" memory would tell you that *gas* is pronounced *gesh,* with a soft *sh* sound. Of course, you would also be using the Substitute Word *you* thought of—the one that would remind you of the proper pronunciation *because* you thought of it. That's why our helping with suggestions for Substitute Words is not really helping you—you might have used **gash** instead of **gas.**

At this point, why don't you try something? Go back to the first examples of foreign words and *really* form the associations. Then see if you know the words and their meanings by filling in these blanks. Don't worry about spelling—when you're in a foreign country, you need the pronunciations and meanings, not the spelling.

FRENCH: father _____   grapefruit _____

                        bridge _____

PORTUGUESE: handkerchief _____   clams _____

                father _____   strawberry _____

                walnut _____   socks _____

                peach _____   dinner _____

                skirt _____   purse _____

Now try it this way (without looking at the above, of course):

noz means _____   peúgas means _____

bolsa means _____   pont means _____

lenço means _____   père means _____

morango means _____   jantar means _____

pai means _____   amejues means _____

pamplemousse means _____ pêssego means _____

saia means _____

If you missed a few, simply go back and strengthen those particular associations. Then test yourself again. Most likely, you'll get them all.

The method is applicable under any circumstances. If the English equivalent is not tangible, you can use a Substitute Word or phrase for that English equivalent. The Siamese word for August is *singhakom*. Ordinarily, August is difficult to picture, because it's intangible. But a **gust** of wind blowing over a **singing comb** is not. See that picture, and you've got it.

The system will work even if a foreign word contains sounds that we don't often use in English (like the soft *sh* in Portuguese). The word for *squirrel* in both French and German contains unfamiliar sounds. In German, the word is *Eichhörnchen;* the *ch* is a back-of-the-throat, guttural sound—almost as if you're clearing your throat. We do not use that sound in English, yet the system applies. **I horn kin** might remind you of *Eichhörnchen;* or, perhaps, **I corn kin**. Use either one for your Substitute phrase, but be sure you get a squirrel into your picture. To help you not just approximate the pronunciation but pronounce the word correctly, you might add clearing your throat to your picture.

The French word for *squirrel* is *écureuil*. We do not have the *euil* sound in English. But **egg cure oil** can certainly get you close to the pronunciation of that difficult word. You might picture a squirrel laying a sick egg, and it cures the egg with oil.

The Greek word for *scissors* is *psalidi*. The *p* is pronounced. Associate **pass a lady** to scissors, and you'll have memorized both the pronunciation of the foreign word *and* its meaning.

The grammar of a language will usually fall into place as you learn the vocabulary, although the system is applicable to any kind of word. It is also applicable to phrases—why shouldn't it be, since phrases are made up of words? The French phrase *rien de grave* is idiomatic for *It's nothing* or *It's nothing serious*. Associate **ran the grave** to **It's nothing** in some ridiculous way, and you've memorized it.

When you fly to a foreign country, you're usually armed with a money converter and a "conversation" booklet in that language. What you see in those booklets is the English equivalent, followed by the foreign translation. The translation is then spelled phonetically (as we did with the Portuguese examples) to give you the pronunciation.

All very well. Only, when you arrive, you end up searching through the booklet (feeling like an idiot), trying to find a word or phrase whenever you want to understand or be understood. Nowhere in these booklets does it tell you how to *remember* the words, phrases, pronunciations, and meanings.

What we're interested in is having you spend the six-plus hours on a transatlantic flight with such a booklet, only *remem-*

bering enough so that when you disembark you'll be able to ask a porter to get your luggage, find you a taxi, tell the taxi driver where to go, etc. And to remember enough, during that flight, to help you through a few weeks' stay. Apply what you're learning here, and you will do just that.

Obviously, you'll learn more if you also apply the systems during your stay. And we're assuming you are neither a linguist nor are you determined to speak like a native. (The systems are extremely helpful for those people, too, but we're concerned at the moment with those who would simply like to make their way more easily during a visit to a foreign country.)

The Portuguese examples were used to teach you the idea, in a language that isn't familiar to many Americans. Here are a few examples in French—really, a mini in-flight French lesson.

If you intend to visit France, you certainly need to be familiar with the French words for many foods. In restaurants heavily patronized by tourists, you may find English translations on the menu—and food that makes you wonder what all the shouting is about when it comes to French cuisine.

In small restaurants, out-of-the-way restaurants, special restaurants, you may not find translations, nor will you find English-speaking waiters—which makes it a little difficult to find out what a word on the menu means.

We asked four volunteers who had no knowledge of the French language (but some knowledge of our systems) to apply the systems to the following words. In less than twenty minutes, they all knew the English meaning when we said the French word, and vice versa. See if you can do it in that time. The *only* way to do it that quickly is to think of pictures for the suggestions and really see them.

Bread—*pain (pan)*. The handle of a **pan** is a loaf of French bread.

Butter—*beurre (buhr)*. A large bar of butter is full of **burrs**.

Mushrooms—*champignons (shahn-peen-yawn)*. A gigantic mushroom delivers a monstrous, **champion yawn.**

Beans—*haricots (ah-ree-koh)*. Millions of beans are wearing **hairy coats.**

Chicken—*poulet (poo-leh)*. You're **pulling** the **leg** of a gigantic chicken.

Watermelon—*pastèque (pass-tehk)*. A gigantic watermelon **passes** a **deck** of cards to you.

Snails—*escargots (ess-cahr-go)*. A gigantic snail is carrying a cargo of S's—**S cargo**

Ham—*jambon (zhan-bown)*. You **jam** a **bone** into a gigantic ham.

Duck—*canard (ka-nar)*. Someone throws a **can hard,** and you duck.

Lobster—*homard (oh-mar)*. Your mother is disguised as a lobster; you say, "**Oh, Ma.**"

Water—*l'eau (low)*. You go under the table (**low**) to drink water.

Garlic—*ail (eye)*. A gigantic piece of garlic (smell it) falls in your **eye.**

Cake—*gâteau (gah-toh)*. A gigantic birthday cake has **got** you by the **toe.**

Ice cream—*glace (glas)*. You're eating **glass** instead of ice cream.

Check—*l'addition (lah-dish-yawn)*. A **dish yawns** as it hands you the check.

Tip—*pourboire (poor-bwahr)*. You tip over a **poor boy.**

Look at them once again, and go over (see) your associations.

Bread—*pain (pan)*	Butter—*beurre (buhr)*
Mushrooms—*champignons (shahn-peen-yawn)*	Beans—*haricots (ah-ree-koh)*
Chicken—*poulet (poo-leh)*	Watermelon—*pastèque (pass-tehk)*
Snails—*escargots (ess-cahr-go)*	Ham—*jambon (zhan-bown)*
Duck—*canard (ka-nar)*	Lobster—*homard (oh-mar)*
Water—*l'eau (low)*	Garlic—*ail (eye)*
Cake—*gâteau (gah-toh)*	Ice cream—*glace (glas)*
Check—*l'addition (lah-dish-yawn)*	Tip—*pourboire (poor-bwahr)*

Now, either test yourself or have someone else test you.

Remember to apply the system to phrases just as you do to words. The French for *How much is it?* is *Combien est-ce?* (*kawn-byen-ehss*). You see a comb that can change and be an S (**comb be an S**); you want it, so you ask how much it is. "**Come be an ass**" would also do. Of course, if you only say *"Combien?"* the merchant will know what you mean. Picture yourself asking how much it costs to **comb Ben**. When you get the answer, you may want to say, "That's too much" (or too expensive): *C'est trop cher (seh-troh-shehr)*—you want to **sit** and **row** in a **chair**, but it's much too expensive.

Please: s'il vous plaît (seel-voo-pleh). Picture a seal playing by yelling "Boo"; you ask it to please stop. **Seal boo play** will remind you of *s'il vous plaît*.

I need: il me faut (eel-muh-foh). A gigantic eel is your foe (**eel my foe**) and coming to hurt you—you need help.

If some of the Substitute Words or thoughts used as examples seem farfetched to you, make up your own. But it doesn't matter if they're farfetched; they'll still serve as reminders. If you try to actually see the suggested pictures, you'll see that they serve quite well.

Except for *l'eau* and *l'addition,* we've omitted the articles, which in many languages are "masculine" or "feminine." In French, *le* is masculine, *la* is feminine, and *les* is plural for either gender. All you really need is a standard for one of them. For example, you might decide to use singing (**la, la**) as the standard for the feminine article. Any picture that has singing in it tells you that the item is feminine; if it doesn't have singing in it, the item is masculine. Or, see a dress on any noun that takes the feminine article.

For example, take *table* (pronounced *tabluh*). That's a word you won't need a Substitute for because it's spelled exactly like the English equivalent, *table*. Let's assume you *do* want to remember whether it's masculine or feminine. If you picture a table singing to you, and singing is the standard you've chosen for feminine, you won't forget that *table* is *la* table, not *le* table. On the other hand, *restaurant* (another easy one) is masculine because the restaurant you picture *doesn't* sing.

An English word that you never heard before is really the same as a foreign word; it's foreign to you, anyway. Apply the system in exactly the same way. The English word *peduncle* means a flower stalk. See yourself having **paid** your **uncle** with flower stalks instead of money, and you have both a reminder of the pronunciation of the new word and its meaning.

The *omphalos* is the navel or belly button. Omphalos sounds like **arm fell loose.** See this picture: Your arm fell loose—where did it fall? Right into your belly button, of course.

A *factotum* is a handyman. Picture a handyman (whatever that conjures up in your mind) painting **facts** on a **totem** pole.

If you're a crossword-puzzle nut, you'd save time if you remembered that the clue "sun god" usually refers to *Ra.* Picture the sun cheering, "**rah,**" and you'll probably never have to look it up again. The clue "Chinese pagoda" usually refers to *taa.* Associate pagoda to **tar,** and you'll have your reminder.

The idea applies to any kind of terminology. To a medical student, the Substitute Word for femur could be **fee more**; for sacrum, **sack rum**; for patella, **pat Ella**; hypoglossal, a **glossy hypodermic** needle; and so on.

A pharmaceutical student might picture someone putting a large **bell down** over his head as he **throws pine** trees from under it—to remember that atropine (I throw pine) comes from the belladonna (bell down) root or leaf.

As with the foreign words, if you go back a bit and really form the associations for the English words (instead of just reading passively) you should be able to fill in these blanks easily:

The sun god is _____.   A Chinese pagoda is a _____.

A factotum is a _____.   A peduncle is a _____.

The omphalos is the _____.   Atropine comes from the _____ root or leaf.

It might interest you to know that, as far back as the 1600's, children were taught language by means of pictures and pictures in the mind. It must have worked pretty well—think of all the people then who could speak Latin, Greek, and other languages.

There's one point that should be stressed: We have yet to find the memory problem that the systems taught in this book can't make easier to handle. You'll see that, with a slight twist or manipulation, the systems must apply. It doesn't matter how difficult the problem is; in fact, the more difficult the problem, the more valuable the systems.

When we teach students how to remember foreign language vocabulary, there's usually one who'll say, "Great, but what about languages like Chinese?" Well, what about them? Of course it's more difficult to learn Chinese or Japanese than French or Spanish—but it always will be, whether or not you use our systems. Applying the systems will still make the chore less of a chore, and take the drudgery out of what can be enjoyable.

If we show a student how to remember things in sequence, and he says, "Okay, but I have hundreds of things I must remember in sequence," his thinking is a bit inverted. It's *because* he has hundreds of things to remember that he *needs* the systems. If he had only four things to remember, he wouldn't need them at all.

8 NAMES AND FACES

JL: I had agreed to help one of Coach Woody Hayes's football players with his studies, so I went over to the player and said, "Hi, I'm Jerry Lucas—what's your name?" He didn't say anything for maybe a half a minute, just seemed to be rapidly counting on his fingers. Then he said, "Bob." I heard him, but I was curious. "I'm sorry," I said, "what did you say your name was?" He went through the same routine again, before finally saying, "Bob." Of course, I had to ask him why he did that.

"Well," he said, "I have a terrible memory—I even find it hard to remember my own name. So, what I do is sing to myself, keeping time on my fingers, 'Happy birthday to you, happy birthday to you, happy birthday, dear . . . *Bob!*"

HL: That's about the best "worst memory" story I've ever heard. It reminds me of the late Richard Himber, the musician and magician, who was a good friend of mine. During the early years, when I was first starting, he was going to get me on the "Ed Sullivan Show."

He dragged me to the studio during a rehearsal and cornered Sullivan. "Ed," he said, "this guy is fantastic. He'll meet everyone in your audience. Then, during the show, he'll call each person's name. As he does, each person will stand up—until the *entire audience* is standing!" As was often the case with Dick he had it mixed up—all the people I've met stand, then *sit down* as I call their names.

Anyway, Sullivan looked at Dick for a moment, and said, "I can have the band play 'The Star-Spangled Banner' and get the same result!"

JL: Well, *he* could get things mixed up too. One year I was named *Sports Illustrated* Sportsman of the Year, and the announcement was to be made on the Sullivan show—you know, Ed was to introduce me from the audience.

So, near the end of the show, he says, "Ladeez and gentlemen, we have in our audience the *Sports Illustrated* Sportsman of the Year. Would you please give a big welcome to Mr. Jerry . . . *Lewis!*"

•

Most of us recognize faces (did you ever hear anyone say, "Oh, I know your name, but I don't recognize your face"?). It's the names we have trouble with. Since we do usually recognize faces, the thing to do is apply a system wherein the face *tells* us the name. That is basically what our system accomplishes, if it is applied correctly.

The first problem is the name. Well, that one is easily solved —simply apply the Substitute Word system of memory. You won't need it for many names that already have meaning— names like Hayes, Howe, Carpenter, Fox, Paige, Coyne, Paynter, Gold, or Knott immediately create pictures in your mind.

Other names may not have meaning, but will still remind you of something tangible. For example, the names Hudson, Jordan, and Shannon will probably make you think of a river, and the name Ruth might make you think of baseball.

The vast majority of names, however, have no meaning at all. They are conglomerations of sound, just like a word in a foreign language. That's where the Substitute Word system comes in.

Before we give you some examples, you should be aware of

the fact that most people don't really forget names. They just don't remember them in the first place—often, they don't really *hear* them in the first place. Just think back and remember the many times you've been introduced to someone, when all you heard was a mumble. There's no way on earth to remember a mumble!

For some reason, people are usually embarrassed to simply say, "I'm sorry, I didn't hear your name." There's nothing to be embarrassed about. Since a person's name is one of his most prized possessions, it's flattering to make even the slightest fuss over it. Asking him to repeat it shows that you're interested enough in him to want to be sure you get his name right.

Then there are those who don't bother asking the person to repeat his name because they feel that they'll probably never meet him again, so what difference does it make? Of course, they often do meet that person again—which is why half the world seems to address the other half as Darling, Buddy, Fella', Mac, Champ, Honey, or Sweetheart. Not because "Honey" is so special to them, but because they don't know who in blazes they're talking to! Which is probably all right, because the chances are that "Honey" and "Buddy" don't know who *they're* talking to, either!

Anyway, if you would like to remember names and faces, there are three steps involved; the first step takes care of the name, the second takes care of the face, and the third locks the two of them together. What you have to do is associate the name *to* the face in some ridiculous way. But for now, let's talk about the first step, remembering the name.

Ordinarily, there'd be no way to picture a name like Bentavagnia (pronounced *bent-a-vane-ya*). But you *can* picture, say, a bent weather vane. And **bent vane** has to remind you of Bentavagnia!

The Substitute Word system will work beautifully to help you remember names. Applying it will *force* you to listen to, pay attention to, concentrate on that name—to be Originally Aware of it. You can't come up with a Substitute Word for a mumble. You simply *must* be sure to hear the name, even if you have to ask the person to repeat it.

Before you learn how to attach a Substitute Word to a face, you should be convinced that there is no name, no matter how long or odd-sounding, for which you cannot find a Substitute Word, phrase, or thought. It might even be a thought you can't put into words. But you'll always be able to think of something that can be pictured, and that will remind you of the name.

The name Antesiewicz seems formidable. But it's pronounced *ante-sevage*, and it's easy enough to picture **anti-savage** or **Auntie save itch**. Suddenly, the name seems less formidable. Pukczyva (pronounced *puk-shiva*) is another name that ordinarily would go in one ear and out the other because, subconsciously or consciously, you'd think, "I'll never remember that, anyway—why try?" And, of course, you'd be right; you'd never remember it. But if you picture a hockey **puck shiver**ing because it's on ice, you can picture that name.

For the name Barclay, you could use **bar clay** or **bark lay**; for Smolenski, a **small lens** (camera) skiing; for Caruthers, a **car** with **udders**; for Krakowitz, **cracker wits**; for Frankesni, **frank** (hot dog) **has knee**; for Esposito, **expose a toe**; for Dalrymple, **doll rumple**; for Kolodny, **colored knee**; for Androfkavitz, **Ann drop car witch**; for Giordano, **jawed on O**; for Virostek, **virile stick**; and so on.

The Substitute Word or phrase you use needn't contain all the exact sounds of the name; cover the main sound or elements, and you'll have the reminder you need. "True" memory will fill in the rest for you.

As with most anything else, it will become easier and easier as you practice applying the idea. You'll develop standards for certain names, prefixes, suffixes, and even sounds. Here are three standards we mention to our students: For Smith, always picture a blacksmith's hammer; for Cohen, an ice cream **cone**; for Gordon, a **garden**.

For the suffix -*son*, you might always see a smaller version of the main thing you're picturing. For example, for Robinson, you could see a **robin** and a smaller robin—its **son**. Or, you could use the **sun** in the sky as your standard. For *Mc*- or *Mac*-, you could always picture a **Mack** truck; for -*itz* or -*witz*, picture brains (**wits**); for -*berg*, see an ice**berg**; for -*stein*, picture a beer **stein**; for -*ton*, see the item weighing a **ton**; for a -*ger* ending, we usually picture either a wild animal growling (**grr**), or a **cigar**.

Once you use something for any name, prefix, suffix, etc., you'll probably use it automatically when you hear that sound again—it will become a standard to you.

Here's a list of nearly six hundred of the most common names in America, plus suggestions for Substitute Words or phrases for each of them. (Names that already have meaning, like Storm, Bell, Paine, Brown, Wolfe, etc., are not listed.) Take the time to go over these at least once; some standards will start forming for you. You can use the list as a drill, if you like. Cover the Substitute Word suggestions with your hand or a piece of paper, and see if you don't come up with some of the same words or phrases we've listed. It will help you become more familiar with the idea, and it's a good imagination exercise.

Aarons	run on air, air runs
Abbott	an abbott, I bought
Abrams	rams, ape rams
Abramson	ram son
Adams	fig leaf, Adam's apple, a dam
Adler	paddler, add law
Alexander	lick sand, lick sander
Allen	alley, all in
Altman	old man
Anderson	hand and son

Andrews .... Ann draws, Ann drools
Anthony .... hand ton, Mark Anthony
Applebaum .... apple bum
Archer .... archer, ah chair
Arnold .... arm old
Ashburn .... ash burn
Atkins .... hat kin
Atkinson .... hat kin son

Bailey .... bale E
Baldwin .... bald one, bald win
Barnett .... bar net
Barry .... bury, berry
Bartley .... bought lay, barred lea (meadow)
Barton .... bar ton
Bauer .... bower
Baxter .... back stir, backs tear
Beck .... back, peck
Bennett .... bend net, bend it, Tony
Benson .... bend son
Bentley .... band lay, English car
Berman .... bar man (bartender)
Bernstein .... burn stein
Blair .... blare, lair
Blake .... flake, lake
Borden .... milk, boarding
Bowen .... bowing
Boyd .... bird
Bradley .... brad lay
Brady .... braid E
Brent .... rent, bent
Brewster .... brew stir, rooster
Brody .... broad E
Bruce .... ruse, bruise

Bryant	buy ant, buoyant
Buckley	buckle
Burke	berg, perk
Burton	buy ton, burr ton
Callahan	call a hand
Cameron	camera on
Campbell	soup, camp bell
Carroll	Christmas carol, carry all
Carson	car son, Johnny
Carter	car tear, cart her
Chadwick	shadow wick, chat wick
Chandler	chandelier
Chapman	chapped man, chop man
Charles	char, quarrels
Chester	chest tear, jester
Chilton	chill ton
Chisholm	chisel
Christenson	Christian son
Christopher	Christ go far
Clark	clock, clerk
Clinton	clean ton
Cochran	rooster (cock) ran
Coleman	cold man, coal man
Collier	collar, call ya'
Collins	collie, Tom Collins
Connolly	con a lay
Connor	counter, con her
Cooper	chicken coop, coo pair
Craig	crack
Crandall	ran doll, crane doll
Crawford	crawl Ford, Joan
Crawley	crawl lay, Raleigh
Crosby	cross bee, Bing

Crowley	crow lay
Cunningham	cunning ham
Curtis	curt, Tony
Daley	daily, day
Daniels	Dan yells
Davis	Davis cup (tennis)
Davison	Davis cup and son
Dawson	door son
Denton	dent ton
Deutsch	touch, German
Dixon	Dick (Tracy) son
Donahue	don a hue (color)
Donald	Duck, darn old
Donovan	don a van
Doran	door ran
Dougherty	dough in tea, dock her tea
Douglas	dug glass, dug less
Doyle	doily, toil, oil
Driscoll	drizzle
Dudley	dud lay, dead lay
Duffy	the fee
Dugan	do again, due again
Duncan	dunkin'
Dunlap	down lap, down lip
Dunn	dun, down
Dutton	button, the ton
Dwyer	wire, dryer
Eaton	eat ton, eatin'
Eberhardt	ever hard
Edelman	a dull man
Edwards	wards (off)
Egan	he can, again

Ehrlich .... air lick, oil lick
Elliott .... lot, L E hot
Ellis .... L ass, Alice
Engle.................... angle, and gull
Epstein .... ebb stein
Evans .... heavens

Farber .... far bar, far bear
Farrell................. far rail, barrel
Feinberg .... fine berg
Feldman .... fell man
Ferguson............. fur go son
Feuer................... foyer, fire
Finney................. fishy, fini
Flanagan............. fan again
Fleming .... flaming, lemming
Fletcher .... fetch her, lecher
Flynn................... flyin', Errol
Foley .... fall E, foal
Forbes .... four bees, orbs
Forman .... boss, four men
Forrester............. forest, forest tear
Foster .... forced her
Frazer .... freezer, raise her
Freedman .... free man, reed man
Fried .... freed
Friedlander......... free land
Fuller .... full, brush

Gallagher .... gal
Gardner .... gardener
Garrison .... carry son
Gaynor .... gain her
Geller .... gala, gal law, kill her

Gelman	kill man
Gerber	go bare, baby food
Gibson	vodka gibson, give son
Gilbert	kill bed
Ginsberg	gin berg
Gladstone	glad stone
Gleason	glee son, Jackie
Goodwin	good win
Gorman	gore man, doorman
Graham	cracker, gray ham
Gregory	gory, Peck, gray gory
Griffin	grip fin
Griffith	grip fish
Grover	rover, grow
Gulliver	giant, gull liver
Gunther	gun tore, gunned her
Hahn	hone
Hamilton	hammer ton
Hansen	hansom cab, handsome
Harper	harp, hopper
Harrington	herring ton, her ring ton
Harris	harass, hairy
Harrison	hairy son
Hartman	heart man, hard man
Haupt	hopped, hoped
Healey	heal E
Heller	hello
Helman	hell man, held man
Henderson	hen son
Hendricks	hen tricks, hand tricks
Henry	hen
Herman	her man
Hicks	hicks, hiccups

Hirsch .... Hershey bar
Hirshfeld .... Hershey fell
Hobart .... whole bar, hope hard
Hodges .... hedges
Hoffman .... huff man, half man
Hogan .... hoe can, whole can
Holden .... hold in, hold den
Hollis .... hollers
Holt .... halt, hold
Hooper .... hoop
Hopkins .... hop kin
Hornsby .... horns bee
Horowitz .... horror wits
Houlihan .... hold a hand, hooligan
Houston .... house ton, use ton
Howard .... how hard
Hoyle .... hurl, oil
Hubbard .... Old Mother (Hubbard), hop hard
Hughes .... hues, use, ewes
Hyman .... high man

Isaacs .... eye sacks, ice axe
Israel .... is real, Star of David

Jackson .... jack son
Jacobs .... cobs, Jacob's ladder
Jaffe .... café, coffee
James .... aims
Jansen .... Sen Sen, *ja*nitor's son
Jerome .... chair roam
Johnson .... john son, Lyndon, yawn son
Jones .... owns, john

Kagan .... K again

Kahn	can, con
Kaiser	guy sore, geyser
Kantor	cantor, can't tear
Kaufman	cough man
Keegan	key can
Keller	call her, kill her, color
Kelly	call E, kill E, green
Kennedy	can a day, can of D's
Kenny	can knee, penny
Kent	can't, canned
Kerr	car, cur
Kessler	cast law
Klein	climb, K line
Knapp	nap, knapsack
Koenig	king, K nick, coin nick
Kornfeld	corn fell
Kramer	gray Ma, creamer
Krieger	regal, cry gore
Lafferty	laugh tea
Lambert	lamb butt
Lang	long
Langer	longer, languor, linger
Larkin	lark in, lark kin
Larson	arson, larceny
Lawrence	law ants, lower ants
Lawson	law son
Lawton	law ton
Lederman	leader man, letter man
Lee	lea
Lehman	layman
Leonard	lean hard
Leslie	less lie
Lester	less tear, jester

Levine	the vine, live in
Levinson	level son, leavin' son
Levy	levee, Levi's
Lewis	lose, loose, who is
Lieberman	labor man, leave her man
Lindsey	lint sea, lindy hop
Logan	low can, low again
Loughran	lock ran
Lund	land
McCarthy	Mack cart tea
McCoy	me coy, decoy
McDonald	Mack and Duck (Donald)
McGee	my key
MacLeod	Mack loud, Mack cloud, my cloud
McMann	Mack man
Mahoney	Ma hold knee, my whole knee, my honey
Malone	alone
Manning	man ink, manning
Marcus	mark us
Marshall	marshal, Ma shall
Martin	Ma tin, mar tin
Mason	mason, my son
Maxwell	makes well, mix well
Mayer	mayor
Mead	meat, meet
Merrill	merry ill
Metcalf	met calf
Meyer	mire, my ear
Michaels	mike calls, mike kills
Middleton	middle ton
Mitchell	shell, mitt shell
Monroe	man row, Marilyn
Moore	moor, more

Moran	Ma ran, more ran
Morgan	more can
Morris	Morris chair, Ma is, more rice
Morse	moss
Morton	mutton, more ton
Muller	mulling it over
Murphy	my fee, more fee, morphine
Nash	gnash
Neill	kneel
Nelson	kneel son, wrestling hold
Nichols	nickels
Nixon	mix on, nicks on
North	storm, wind, compass
Norton	no ton
Nussbaum	nose bum, nuts bum
O'Brien	oh burn, brine
Ogden	egg den, egged on
Oliver	olive
Olsen	old son
O'Neal	kneel, O kneel
Oppenheim	open home
Owens	owes, owns
Padgett	patch it, page it
Paley	pale, pail
Palmer	palm, palm Ma
Parkington	parking ton
Patrick	pat trick
Patterson	pat a son
Paul	pull, pall
Pawley	pulley, pull E
Paxton	packs ton

Pearce .... pierce
Pearson .... pierce son, pear son
Perkins .... perking
Perlman .... pearl man
Perlmutter .... pearl mutter
Perry .... bury, pear
Peters .... peters out, fades, P tears
Phillips .... full lips
Pincus .... pin cushion, pink ass, pink S
Powell .... dowel, towel, power, Pa well

Quinn .... win

Rafferty .... rap for tea
Raleigh .... roll lea, raw lea, roll E
Randall .... ran doll
Rappaport .... rap on port
Ratner .... rat knee, rat on her
Raymond .... ray on mount, rain mount
Reiss .... rise, rice
Resnick .... rest nick
Reynolds .... ran old, rain old, rain holds
Rhodes .... roads
Richards .... rich
Rigney .... rig knee
Riley .... rye lea, rile E
Roberts .... robbers
Robeson .... robe son
Rogers .... Buck Rogers, roger (affirmative)
Rosen .... rose in
Rosenberg .... rose in (ice)berg
Ross .... rose, raws
Roth .... wrath
Rubin .... ruby

Ruppert .... rope pat, rude pit
Russell................. rustle, wrestle
Rutherford .... rode a Ford, rudder Ford
Ryan .... cryin', rind, Rhine

Samuels............... some mules
Satenstein .... satin stein
Sawyer .... saw ya'
Saxon.................. sacks on
Scher .... chair, share, sheer
Schmidt.............. blacksmith's hammer, shy mitt
Schneider .... she neither
Schoenberg......... shine (ice)berg, shone berg
Schultz .... shields, shoots
Schuster .... shoe stir, shoe store
Schwartz............. warts
Scott .... scotch, Scot
Sears .... burns (sears), Sears Roebuck
Seiden .... side in
Seward .... steward, seaward
Sexton .... sacks ton, sexy ton
Shaeffer.............. shave four, shaver, beer
Shaw .... shore, pshaw
Shay .... shade, say, shave
Sheehan .... sheen
Shelton .... shell ton, shelter
Sherman .... show man, sure man
Siegel .... sea gull, see gal
Simmons .... simmers, see man, mattress
Simon .... sigh man, Simple
Simpson .... simple son, simper son
Sitron .... sit run
Skidmore............. skid more
Slade .... slayed, slate

Sloan .... loan, slow
Slocum .... slow comb
Snead .... need, snood, Sammy
Solomon .... wise man, solo man, solemn man
Sommers .... summers
Spector .... spectator, ghost, inspector
Spencer .... expense her, pins her, pen sore
Squire .... wire, square, choir
Stacey .... stay see, tasty
Sterling .... silver, starling
Stern .... stern (father figure)
Stevens .... stevedore, steep fins
Stewart .... steward
Sullivan .... John L., sold a van
Sussman .... shush man
Swanson .... swan son
Sweeney .... sweet knee

Talmadge .... tall midget, tall Madge
Tate..................... tight, tea ate
Taub .... daub, tub
Teitelbaum .... titled bum
Terry................... cloth (towel), tear E
Thatcher .... that chair, thatcher
Thomas .... tom tom, tom ask
Thompson........... tom tom son, thump son
Tipton................. tip ton
Tobias .... toe bias, toe buy us
Todd .... toddle, toddy
Tracy................... trace E
Travers .... travels, traverse
Treadway .... tread, dread way
Trent................... rent
Tucker .... tuck 'er, tuck car

Tuttle .... turtle
Tyler .... tiler, tile her

Udall .... you doll
Unger .... hunger

Victor .... winner, Vic tore
Vincent .... win cent

Wagner .... wag her, wagoner
Wallace............... wall lace, wall is, wall ace
Walsh .... waltz
Walters .... wall tears, falters, Barbara
Warner .... warn her
Warren .... warring, war in
Wasserman .... blood test, water man
Watkins .... watt kin
Watson .... watt son, what son
Watts .... watts, light bulb
Waverly .... wave early, waver lea
Wayne .... wane, John
Weber.................. web, web bar
Webster .... web stir, dictionary
Weeks .... calendar, weak
Weiner .... frankfurter, weenie
Weintraub .... wine trap
Weiss.................. wise
Welch .... grape juice, welsh (on a bet)
Wellington .... well ink ton
Whalen .... whalin', whale, wailing
Whitney .... white knee, whittle knee
Williams .... will yams, yams
Wilson................ will son, whistle
Winston .... wins ton, Churchill

Woolsey .... wool see, we'll see
Worthington........ worth ink ton
Wright .... write

Young .... baby

Zimmer............... simmer
Zuckerman .... sucker man, man with all-day sucker

If you've gone over this list even once, you'll find that many of these Substitute Words will come to mind the next time you hear some of these names. And when you come up with your own Substitute Word or phrase for a name, you're even more likely to remember it whenever you hear the name.

JL: The first time I saw you on television. . . .

HL: I know, you were just a little boy!

JL: Well, not quite. Anyway, I knew something about memory systems, but I'd never heard of anyone remembering four hundred names. I couldn't believe it.

HL: The funny thing is that nobody else believed it—or so it seemed. My first national television exposure was on the original Jack Paar "Tonight Show." He put me on for about eight minutes near the end of the show, and I guess I must have rattled off close to four hundred names in about seven minutes.

Two days later, someone from Paar's office called me. It seems they'd received hundreds of calls, letters, and telegrams to the effect that what I'd done was impossible, no one could remember that many people in so short a time—they must have all been friends of mine!

JL: What did you say to *that?*

HL: I said, "Who the heck has four hundred friends?!"

•

Now for step two. You've just been introduced to someone and you've made up a Substitute Word for his name; what do you do with it? Well, what you have to do is look at that person's face and select what *you* think is its outstanding feature.

You've accomplished one of the two important steps by forcing yourself to be Originally Aware of the name. Now, by searching for an outstanding feature, you're accomplishing the second important step—you're forcing yourself to look at, be interested in, concentrate on, that face!

What you select could be anything: hair or hairline; forehead (narrow, wide, or high); eyebrows (straight, arched, bushy); eyes (narrow, wide-spaced, close-set); nose (large, small, pug, ski); nostrils (flaring, pinched); high cheekbones; cheeks (full or sunken); lips (straight, arched, full, thin); chin (cleft, receding, jutting); lines, pimples, warts, dimples—anything.

First impressions are usually lasting impressions, and what is outstanding on someone's face now will, most likely, seem outstanding when you see that face again. That's important; but more important is the fact that you've really looked at that face. You're etching that face into your memory by just *trying* to apply the system.

What you select may not be what someone else would select, but it will work for you. We all think and see differently—fine, that's as it should be. What *you* see, what you select, is best for you.

All right; you've decided on an outstanding feature, and you already had a Substitute Word for its owner's name. Now we come to step three—you associate the Substitute Word to the outstanding feature. If you do this properly, it will almost be like having the person's name written on his face!

Even if step three didn't work (which it does), just applying steps one and two *must* improve your memory for names and faces, because you've done what most people don't do—you've *paid attention;* you've listened and looked.

But it is step three that gives purpose to steps one and two—it locks the name and face together for you. Form a ridiculous association between your Substitute Word and the outstanding feature of the face; that's all. And, you'll find that it's almost impossible *not* to make the picture ridiculous; it will happen automatically.

Look, you've just met Mr. Crane. A picture of a large crane, as used by construction workers, comes to mind; or perhaps the storklike bird. You've looked at his face and decided that his high forehead is the outstanding feature. You look at that forehead, and *really* picture many large **cranes** flying out of it; or, you can see them attacking that high forehead! Or perhaps the entire forehead is one gigantic **crane**. As with any association, you have many choices as to the kind of picture you visualize. You must be sure—*force* it at first—to really see that picture. The next time you meet Mr. Crane, *you'll know his name!*

If Mr. Bentavagnia has a large nose, you'd see a **bent** weather **vane** where the nose should be. Mr. Pukczyva has bulging eyes; really see those **shivering** hockey **pucks** flying out of his eyes, hitting you in the face. Or, his eyes *are* shivering hockey pucks. Mr. Antesiewicz has a noticeable cleft in his chin. See savages charging at you out of that cleft; you're defending yourself against them—you're **anti-savage**. Mr. Cohen has deep character lines (they used to be called "worry" lines) on his forehead. Picture those lines being dripping ice cream **cones**; or millions of dripping ice cream cones flying out of those lines.

You've just learned the best system for remembering names and faces—and the only one that works for *any* name. (A strong statement, but we'll stand by it!) In our classes, after learning the system, students call off the names of twenty to forty other students, whose names they've heard once—the first time they try it!

You can try it right now, using "word pictures." Five of these were just used as examples. Go back to Mr. Crane, Mr. Bentavagnia, Mr. Pukczyva, Mr. Antesiewicz, Mr. Cohen, and really see those pictures in your mind's eye. For now, since you're trying it without real people or faces, see just the features themselves and the ridiculous associations. Now, meet four more "people" (features and names) and do the same thing.

Mr. Colletti has very thick lips. Picture those lips and see millions of cups of tea or tea bags coming out of them; you're calling one of those cups or bags. Really try to visualize that silly action, and **call a tea** will remind you of Colletti. As always, you can make up your own Substitute Words and pictures. You might want to see yourself tasting the tea, spitting out a mouthful, and saying, "**Call 'at tea**?"

Miss Meisterman has very full cheeks. You might picture a man coming out of each cheek and you stir him. **Me stir man**—Meisterman. See that crazy picture.

Dr. Caruthers has very long, wide sideburns. You might see those sideburns being cars or have cars driving out of them); the cars have udders—you're milking the cars. **Car udders**. See the picture. If you want to remember that this is *Dr.* Caruthers, put something into the picture that will *tell* you so. Make up a standard to represent doctor—a stethoscope, perhaps. As you see yourself milking the cars, picture **stethoscopes** coming out of the udders.

Mr. Ponchatrain has deep creases (character lines) from his nostrils to the corners of his mouth. You can see trains running along those tracks (creases); you punch them. **Punch a train**.

Now, if you've really visualized each of those silly pictures, try to fill in the name for each outstanding feature listed below, without worrying about how the names are spelled. They're not listed in the order in which you "met" the people.

Lines in forehead _____   Full cheeks _____

Large nose _____   Long, wide sideburns _____

Cleft in chin _____   High forehead _____

Bulging eyes _____   Creases, nostrils to mouth _____

Thick lips _____

If you remembered to put "Dr." and "Miss" where they belonged, give yourself an extra couple of mental points.

Doing this with "word pictures" is not as easy as applying the system to real faces. Of course, you could practice with newspaper or magazine pictures. Cut out pictures of faces, make up names, and write the names on the backs of the pictures. The system will work with one-dimensional pictures.

The best way to practice, however, is by applying the system from now on, whenever you meet people. You have nothing to lose, and much to gain. The next time you're at a meeting, a cocktail party—the next time you're with a group—apply the system. You'll probably remember 50 percent more names and faces than you ever have before. And that percentage will increase every time you use the system.

When you do try it at, say, a party, be sure to review the names during the evening. If you've applied the system properly, each time you see one of the faces, the name should spring to mind. That's your review. If you look at one face and the name doesn't come to mind, think about it for a while. If it still doesn't come to you, don't be embarrassed to ask for the name again. Then strengthen your association. When you leave the party, you should be able to say good night to people by name. Try it and see for yourself.

Now, meeting people in groups and remembering their names is one thing, but what if you're in a business where, perhaps, three people a day visit your store, office, showroom —and you don't know when, or if, they'll ever come back? Of course, if they do come back, you'd like to call them by name. Many a sale has been clinched that way.

This is the only instance where we suggest that you write down information. Assume you've met three new people today, and have applied the system you just learned. Later, write those three names down on a pad you keep for just that purpose.

Writing each name is a review. You can't write the name

without thinking of it, and, if you've applied the system, you can't think of the name without the face being conjured up in your mind. That's the way the system works—think of the name and you'll visualize the face; think of the face and you'll visualize the name.

The next day, read those names. Three days later, read them again, and a week later read them once more. Then forget about them. The next time one of those people comes into your place of business, you'll know that person's name!

If you meet, say, three people every business day, you may occasionally be reading (reviewing) fifteen to eighteen names at a time. It takes a few minutes. You have to make the decision—is it worth a few minutes, every once in a while, to be able to remember the names of people who may or may not visit you again? Most people think it is.

Now for some more tips on names and faces.

To remember *titles*, come up with standards like the stethoscope in your picture for *Dr.* Caruthers. You can make up a word to represent any title; then just get it into the picture as a reminder. For judge, picture a gavel; for captain, picture a cap, and so on.

For *first* names, make up a Substitute Word for the name and get it into your picture. Once you make one up for any name, it will become a standard for you. You might use **all in** for Alan, **robber** for Robert, **cherry** for Jerry, **floor ants** for Florence, bride (**marry**) for Mary, **shield** for Sheila, **hairy** for Harry, **gym** for Jim, and so on.

You can put anything you like into your original picture—the person's business affiliation, spouse's name, children's names, hobby, how much money he owes you—whatever. Of course, it will take longer to form the original picture or association, but it would take longer to remember all that information in any case.

Say you meet a Mr. Bill Gordon, who is a sales executive with

United States Steel; his wife's name is Renée; he has a son named Jack; and he plays golf.

Bill Gordon has very bushy eyebrows. When you first meet him, you might see his eyebrows being a **garden**; there are dollar **bill**s growing there. As you talk, you find out the other bits of information. Put them into the picture. See an American flag (**U.S.**) that's made of **steel** growing in the garden. The flag is **selling** something to the flowers in the garden. The flowers start to run; they say, "Want to see me **run, eh?**" (Renée). Hydraulic **jacks** (Jack) are also running in the garden—they're swinging **golf** clubs.

It takes time and space to explain these pictures; thinking or visualizing them takes much less time, and you do it during your initial conversation. Don't lose sight of the fact that *trying* to form these ridiculous pictures is forcing you to be Originally Aware; you're registering that information in the first place. Also, remember that after you've used the information a few times, whether it's just the name or information about a person—it all becomes knowledge and the ridiculous pictures fade; they're no longer necessary.

Some final points: Yes, you'll be using high foreheads, big noses, bushy eyebrows, over and over again. Don't worry about it—in remembering the name of every person in an audience, we may use as many as thirty high foreheads! The system still works. It still works because, again, you've had to look at that face with interest, attention, and concentration in order to decide that the forehead is the outstanding feature. That's what really makes the system work. Similarly, it doesn't matter if you always use a blacksmith's hammer to remind you of Smith, Smythe, and Schmidt. You'll know the difference because you had to listen carefully in order to apply the system.

Occasionally, a student will tell us that he or she met someone who had no outstanding feature. That's almost impossible, particularly after you've been using the system for a while—because you'll be noticing and observing more. But if, at first, this seems to be a problem, decide on one feature to use in all such cases. Perhaps you'll always use the nose, if you find no outstanding features. The system will still work because you still have to really *look* at that face in order to decide that it has no outstanding feature.

You might try something now. Turn back to the list of features used in the "word pictures." If you made the associations originally, you'll still know the name that goes with each outstanding feature.

9 ABSENTMINDEDNESS

JL: When I played basketball in high school, I had a teammate named Bob Cole—really one of the greatest shooters I've ever seen, before or since. Trouble was, Bob had a tendency to be absentminded.

He was a starter, of course, and at one game I remember we'd finished our warm-up and were all standing around the coach, ready to go out on the floor. We started to pull off our long warm-up pants; Bob pulled his off, and he had nothing on under them—I mean, *nothing!* He'd forgotten to put on his uniform, and didn't know he was stark naked until he heard all the giggles!

HL: That's embarrassing, of course, but in most cases absentmindedness is annoying, really aggravating. And it's not a problem that has much to do with intelligence. We've all heard of the absentminded professor who winds up the cat, puts his wife out for the night, and kisses the alarm clock good night! And he's intelligent.

JL: On the other hand, I know "idiot savants"—people with fantastic memories who are really *dumb.* Which further supports the idea that intelligence isn't necessarily a factor in memory.

HL: Misplacing something means not remembering where you placed it. When you don't know if you locked your door, you don't *remember* whether or not you locked it—absentmindedness is basically a memory problem.

You are absentminded when your mind is absent; when you perform actions unconsciously, without thinking. We've discussed the difference between seeing and observing—we see with our eyes, but we observe with our minds. If your mind is "absent" when performing an action, there can be no observation; more important, there can be no Original Awareness.

Absentmindedness is probably the most widespread of minor self-annoyances. Although it plagues most of us, it seems particularly to affect the elderly. The techniques we'll discuss here have succeeded in eliminating absentmindedness for countless people, including the elderly.

To some readers, absentmindedness may seem to be a trivial problem. Perhaps they don't realize how much time, energy, and aggravation they spend on searching for items they "just put down for a moment," or on worrying about whether they have turned off the oven, locked the door, unplugged the iron, or on retrieving items they have left in trains, buses, cars, offices, and friends' homes.

The solution to the problem of absentmindedness is both simple and obvious: All you have to do is to be sure to think of what you're doing *during the moment in which you're doing it.* That's all, but obviously it's easier said than done. How can you be sure to *force* yourself to think of a minor action at the moment you're doing it?

There's only one way, and that is by using association. Since association forces Original Awareness—and since being Originally Aware is the same as having something register in your mind in the first place, at the moment it occurs—then forming an instant association must solve the problem of absentmindedness.

You're writing at your desk and the phone rings. As you reach for the phone, you place the pencil behind your ear, or in your hair. The phone call is finished—that took only a few minutes—but now you waste time searching for the pencil that's perched behind your ear. Would you like to avoid that aggravation? All right, then; the next time the phone rings and you start to place the pencil behind your ear, make a fast mental picture in your mind. Actually "see" the pencil going *into* your ear—all the way.

The idea may make you shudder, but when you think of that pencil, you'll know where it is. That silly association of seeing the pencil go into your ear *forced* you to think of two things in a fraction of a second: 1) the pencil, and 2) where you were putting it. Problem solved!

Solved, that is, if you make an association each time you put down your pencil, wherever you put it. Just make it a habit. Keep the idea in mind the first few times, force yourself to form the associations, and after that it *will* become habitual.

If you place your eyeglasses on your television set as you leave your living room, "see" the antenna of the television set going right through the eyeglass lens, shattering it. This association is made without breaking stride, as you walk. We'll guarantee that the next time you think of your glasses, you'll know where they are. For two reasons: First, you *thought* about it when you put them down; and second, the thing that made you think about it, the association, also reminds you of where they are.

If you placed the eyeglasses on your bed, you can picture a gigantic pair of glasses sleeping in your bed. If you stuck them into a pocket, picture the lenses breaking in your pocket and tearing it. Or you're reaching in to get the glasses and your hand is badly cut. All the same idea; the association, no matter what it is, forces you to think of the action at *that* moment. Always do it at the moment; if you put off doing it, you'll forget to form the association and you'll forget where your glasses are!

Many people are plagued by misplacing treasured items. You

usually put the item in a particularly good hiding place—and then never see it again. (If you do, it's likely to be when you move, and empty all your drawers and closets.)

This problem, too, can be solved by making an instant association. Say you have an expensive fountain pen that you want to keep for a child or grandchild. You place it in a drawer beneath your good sweaters for safekeeping. *As* you place it there, see a picture of the pen leaking ink all over those sweaters, ruining them. Be assured that the next time you think of that pen, no matter how long after you've put it away, you'll *know* that it's under your sweaters. You need only associate an item you're putting away to its hiding place once to see that the idea works beautifully.

If you want to be sure not to leave your umbrella at your friend's house, associate umbrella to the last thing you're sure to notice when you leave. If you're wearing a coat, and it's cold outside, you know you won't forget the coat. Associate umbrella to coat; you might see yourself putting on a gigantic umbrella instead of a coat, or using a coat instead of an umbrella to protect you from the rain. The principle is the same—one thing reminds you of the other. If your picture is a clear one, and a ridiculous one, the coat must remind you of the umbrella. If you want to make extra sure, and if you're driving, associate umbrella to your car. You might picture yourself opening the car with an open umbrella instead of a key. Now, if the coat doesn't remind you to take that umbrella, the car certainly will.

Do you often leave your umbrella at the office instead of taking it home? As you arrive and put your umbrella away, associate it to the last thing you normally see or do as you're leaving the office. If you punch a time clock, see yourself placing the umbrella in the slot instead of your card. Or, if you ride an elevator, picture an umbrella operating it. You might also associate the umbrella to something you always see just outside the office building—if one association doesn't remind you to take it with you, the other will remind you to go back and get it.

Perhaps you're one of those people who write an important letter and then forget to take it out of the house and mail it. What's the last thing you do as you leave your house or apartment? Perhaps you check your doorknob to make sure the door is shut, or perhaps you lock the door with a key. Simply associate letter to either doorknob or key—or both. (If you associate letter to, say, doorknob a few times, you probably won't have to do it ever again. *Every* time you look at that knob, it will make you think of letter, and if you've left one inside you'll go back and get it.)

You can always use a second picture as insurance. Perhaps you often take out some garbage when you leave your home. See yourself throwing millions of letters into your garbage can or incinerator.

This will help you remember to take the letter, but you may still leave it in your pocket or purse for a few weeks! One way to avoid that is to hold the letter in your hand until you see a mailbox. Another way is to associate the person or company that the letter is addressed to, to a mailbox. If it's going to someone you can picture or visualize, see that person's head coming out of a mailbox. If it's going to a company, use a Substitute thought. For example, if it's an electric bill, see electricity (lightning) shooting out of a mailbox. In either case, the next time you notice a mailbox—and sooner or later you will—you'll be reminded to take that letter out of your pocket or purse and mail it.

A woman in one of our classes told us that she often burned the roast that she put in the oven because she simply forgot about it. Well, she could avoid this by putting a smaller roast into the oven along with the regular one—when she smelled the small one burning, she'd know the other one was done! The price of meat being what it is, however, there has to be a better way.

Make this a habit—*every* time you put something in the oven, place a small frying pan smack in the center of the kitchen floor! How can you possibly forget about the roast now? Each time you see (or trip over) that frying pan, you'll be reminded of the roast in the oven.

Upon hearing this idea one man said, "That's fine, except that when I put a roast in the oven, I usually go into another room to watch television. Then I can't see the reminder." The solution for him was obvious, of course—to take the frying pan along and put it on top of the television set.

Instead of a frying pan, you can use anything that looks out of place on the floor (or television set): a pot holder, a plate, a hunk of cheese. The idea is based on the standard rule of memory—one thing reminds you of another.

It's not a new idea by any means; it's similar to tying a string on your finger, wearing your watch on the wrong wrist, turning your ring to face the wrong way, or putting a crumpled dollar bill in with your coins. Each of these "out-of-place" things is supposed to remind you of something you want to remember. The problem is that too often they'll remind you that you wanted to remember "something," which isn't much help if you can't remember what the something is. The frying pan on the kitchen floor, on the other hand, must remind you of the roast in the oven because that's all you'll be using it for. If you insist on tying a string around your finger or wearing your watch on the wrong wrist, now you have a way to make it definite. Go ahead and tie the string around your finger, but at the same time be sure to associate whatever it is you want to remember to the string. Now you have the two essentials: first the reminder, then what it is you're being reminded of.

Why ruin your evening out because you spend most of it worrying about whether or not you turned off the oven, locked the door, or unplugged the iron? Form the habit of making a quick association at the moment you do these things. As you shut off the oven, picture yourself (or just your head) in the oven! Really see that picture, and you've consciously thought about the action for a split second. Later on, when you think about the oven, you'll *know* you shut it off.

As you lock your door, see yourself locking it with your head instead of a key. When you unplug your iron, see your head coming out of the socket. The picture you choose is unimportant—*any* picture forces you to think of the action at that moment.

Do you sometimes find yourself going to your refrigerator, opening the door, and then staring inside and wondering what it is you wanted? Just make an association the moment you think of what it is you want from the refrigerator. If you want a glass of milk, see yourself opening the refrigerator door and gallons of milk flying out and hitting you in the face! Try this idea, and you'll never stare into a refrigerator again.

That's all there is to it. It's like grabbing your mind by the scruff of the neck and forcing it to think of a specific thing at a specific moment. Force yourself to do it at first, and it will become habitual before you know it.

Forming these associations may strike you as a waste of time. You won't feel that way once you've tried using the idea. You'll see, after a short while, that the ridiculous pictures are formed in hardly any time at all. Even more important is the time that you'll be *saving*.

•

JL: The "out-of-place" idea has saved me when it comes to getting out of bed in the mornings. You see, if the alarm clock is where it belongs, I'll just reach over with my long arm, shut it off, and go right back to sleep. So I keep it across the room—and whenever I pull out the alarm-set I picture that little knob going right through my thumb, nail and all.

HL: Which forces you to think, at that exact moment, about the fact that you *are* setting the alarm.

JL: I do this every night, and I never have to get out of bed after I'm in to check whether or not I set the clock.

HL: All right. Now, you saw that picture last night, and you'll think of the clock after you're in bed tonight. Does last night's picture ever come back to you, making you think you set the alarm when you actually didn't?

JL: Never has happened. "True" memory tells me the truth. Most important is the Original Awareness. If I *haven't* made the silly picture on any night, I'll know I haven't set the clock.

HL: I know it can't go wrong—I've used it for years, just as I've used the "out-of-place" idea for years to remind me in the morning of something I thought of during the night.

JL: You mean when you've had that million-dollar idea—

HL: Which is usually worth $1.63 in the morning light. Still, I always felt that idea had to be immortalized. So at first I'd put on the lights, find a pad and pencil, and write it down—then, since I invariably woke up my wife, I started keeping a pad on my night table and writing down the idea in the dark.

JL: Could you read your writing in the morning?

HL: Not too well. Which was fine, because that inspired me to really solve the problem. Now, whenever I get an idea, I reach out an arm and do something that will be sure to catch my attention in the morning. Usually, I dump all my cigarettes on the floor—when I get out of bed in the morning I can't miss stepping on those cigarettes and being reminded that I had an idea during the night.

JL: Do you ever have trouble remembering *what* the idea was?

HL: Not usually. But if I do feel I need a reminder of the thought itself—

JL: You associate the Key Word of the idea to cigarettes.

HL: Right! And if I ever manage to stop smoking, I'll reach over and turn my clock face down, or put it on the floor, or push a book off my night table.

JL: Anything that's out of place, that forces you to look at it and think, "What in the world is that doing there?" will do.

•

If you've been applying the systems, you've not only improved your memory, you've improved your sense of imagination, concentration, and *observation*.

By now, you must realize that in order to remember anything, you must pay attention to it—it must be observed. Applying our systems will automatically sharpen your observation.

Having a better sense of observation is almost like taking an "awareness pill." You'll be able to *really* notice, and be aware of, things that ordinarily would make only a vague impression. Most people we've talked to admit that they would have taken an "awareness pill," if there were such a thing, whenever they traveled to new places. After the trip or visit, they never could clearly visualize the beautiful things they'd seen—hadn't *really* noticed or observed them.

All the ideas in this chapter have been intended to force you to pay attention, to observe. You cannot sharpen your observation without applying some effort at first, as is the case with most of the memory systems. But observation, too, will become habit if you practice it consciously and conscientiously.

Up to now, you probably haven't had to expend much effort in learning and applying our systems. Names and faces, errands, foreign words—whatever the memory problem, the solution has largely been a matter of grasping a simple idea and using just a bit of imagination.

But nothing worthwhile comes *too* easily. You're about to embark on some entirely new ideas. Although they remain simple, applying them will take a little more effort on your part—but only until the fundamentals are learned and absorbed.

As you move into remembering the more challenging material that follows, work to apply the systems. You may feel that applying memory systems to it seems like a lot of work. Again, that's thinking negatively. *Any* new art or skill seems difficult and cumbersome at first—but only at first, only until you've grasped the fundamentals of the skill. It is *rote* memory that's really a lot of work—and usually for naught, because it just doesn't work too well or too often. Applying the systems, once you've learned the basics, *must* save you much time and work.

So be sure to take the time to learn the basics that follow. You won't regret it!

10 LONG-DIGIT NUMBERS

918527195216390921 12

A Beautiful Naked Blond Jumps Up and Down

HL: The most difficult category to remember? It has to be numbers.

JL: No question about it. Numbers are completely intangible, they're just designs.

HL: They also happen to be the most important things some people have to remember—addresses, telephone numbers, prices, style numbers, formulas, equations, computer codes, statistics, credit card numbers, and so on.

JL: Those who most need to remember numbers like these have trouble for the same reason most people do—it seems impossible to picture them in the mind.

HL: And, of course, it's not at all impossible to learn to picture numbers, even long ones. Like, say . . .

JL: 91852719521639092112!

•

The problem of remembering numbers, probably the most difficult of all memory chores, can be solved by learning a simple phonetic alphabet, consisting of just ten pairs of digits and sounds. They are not at all difficult to learn, even if you use rote memory—which you won't need to do. We want to eliminate rote, not find uses for it. You'll be given a simple memory aid for each pair, and if you concentrate, you'll probably find that you know them after one reading.

First, to break down the idea for you, there are ten digits in our numerical system: 1, 2, 3, 4, 5, 6, 7, 8, 9, and 0. There are also ten basic *consonant* phonetic sounds. (Technically, of course, there are more than ten, but the ten basic ones will serve our purpose admirably.)

Think of the letters *t* and *d* for a moment. Although they are different letters, and fall in different parts of the alphabet, they make the same phonetic sound. Your vocal apparatus (tongue, teeth, lips) is in exactly the same position when making the *t* sound as when making the *d* sound. The *t* sound is a bit harder than the *d*, that's all. For our purposes, they'll be considered the same.

The rule—the vocal apparatus being in the same position— will hold true for other consonant sounds. For example, although *f* and *v* (and *ph*) are different letters, they form the same phonetic sound; again, the only difference is that one is harder than the other, and, again, your lips, tongue, and teeth are in the same position to form either one.

P and *b* are phonetically the same for our purposes. So are *j*, *sh*, *ch*, and soft *g*—your tongue curls the same way to sound any one of them. The hissing sounds, *s*, *z*, soft *c*, are also the same phonetic sound, and so are *k*, hard *c*, and hard *g*.

All right, then. There are ten of these phonetic sounds, and it is the *sounds* we're interested in, not the letters themselves. All we've done is to pair a sound to each digit, and there are only ten pairs for you to learn. That's the phonetic alphabet. Learn it; once you do, you'll use it for the rest of your life—it will never change. Don't worry now about *how* it will be used; just learn it. It can be useful to you in ways you couldn't imagine.

Pay attention to the memory aids; they're silly but they'll

enable you to learn the phonetic alphabet in minutes. The sound that will represent number 1 will always be the sound made by the letters *t* or *d,* and vice versa. The memory aid, which you'll need for only a short while, is this: A typewritten *t* has *one* downstroke. Think of that for just a moment.

The number 2 will always be represented by the sound made by the letter *n.* The memory aid is: A typewritten small letter *n* has *two* downstrokes. Think of that for a moment.

Number 3 will always be represented by the sound made by the letter *m; 3 = m* and *m = 3.* The small typewritten letter *m* has *three* downstrokes, or you might think of the 3M Corporation. Again, it is the sound we're interested in, not the letter.

Number 4 will always be represented by the sound made by the letter *r.* The simplest memory aid for this is that the word "four" ends with an *r.*

Number 5 will always be represented by the sound of *l.* The memory aid: Spread the *five* fingers of one hand, thumb straight out, and the thumb and forefinger form the letter *l.*

Number 6 will always be represented by the sounds *j, sh, ch,* and soft *g* (as in *gentle);* they all make the same phonetic sound. The memory aid: The digit 6 and a capital letter *j* are almost mirror images ⌐ J.

Number 7 will always be represented by the sounds *k,* hard *c* (as in *cap*), hard *g* (as in *glide*). As the memory aid, you can form a capital *k* with two 7's, one right side up and the other upside down, like this: 𝒦.

Number 8 will always be represented by the sound made by the letters *f* or *v* or the sound *ph.* To help you remember this quickly, an 8 and a handwritten *f* are both made with two loops, one above the other 8 ℓ.

Number 9 will always be represented by the sound made by the letters *p* or *b.* The number 9 and the letter *p* are almost exact mirror images 9 Ρ.

And, finally, the zero (0) will be represented by the hissing sound made by the letters *z, s,* or soft *c* (as in *century*). The memory aid: The first sound in the word "zero" is *z.*

If you've read the last few paragraphs with some degree of concentration, the odds are that you already know all, or most, of them. But look at this chart for a moment:

1 = *t* or *d.* A typewritten small *t* has *one* downstroke.

2 = *n.* A typewritten small *n* has *two* downstrokes.

3 = *m.* A typewritten small *m* has three downstrokes.

4 = *r.* The word fou*r* ends with an *r.*

5 = *l.* The *five* fingers, thumb out, form an *l.*

6 = *j, sh, ch,* soft *g.* A 6 and a capital *j* are almost mirror images ⌊ J.

7 = *k,* hard *c,* hard *g.* You can make a capital *k* with two 7's 𝒦.

8 = *f, v, ph.* An 8 and a handwritten *f* look similar 8 *f.*

9 = *p* or *b.* A 9 and a *p* are mirror images 9 P.

0 = *z, s,* soft *c.* The first sound in the word *z*ero is *z.*

A few rules: The vowels, *a, e, i, o, u,* have no value whatsoever in the phonetic alphabet; they are disregarded. So are the letters *w, h,* and *y.* The only time that *h* is important is when it follows certain consonants, changing the sound. Also, although this is rarely used, the *th* sound will for our purposes be the same as the *t* sound: *th* = 1.

Silent letters are disregarded. The word *knee* would transpose to 2 in the phonetic alphabet, not 72. Remember, we are interested in the sound, not the letter. There is a *k* in that word, but it is silent; it makes no sound and therefore has no value. The word *bomb* transposes to 93, not 939; the last *b* is silent. The beauty of this, if you'll forgive our saying so, is that it doesn't even matter whether or not you pronounce (or read) a word correctly. If you happened to speak with an accent, and pronounced that final *b* in *bomb,* you would transpose that word to 939. But since you'd always pronounce it that way, the system would work just as well for you.

This leads to the rule for double letters. The word *patter* transposes to 914, *not* 9114. Yes, there are two *t*'s in the word, but they are pronounced as one *t*. The word *bellow* would transpose to 95: $b = 9$, $l = 5$; the *ow* has no value. The rule is simple and definite; always consider double letters as making only one sound. (Except, of course, where the two letters are obviously pronounced differently—as in "ac*c*ident." The double *c* here transposes to 70.)

Finally, the letter *x* will almost never be used, but it transposes according to the way it is pronounced in a particular word. In the word *fox* the *f* is 8, and the *x* is 70. (The *x* makes the *ks* sounds in that word.) In the word *complexion*, however, the *x* would transpose to 76. Pronounce *complexion* slowly and you'll see why. As for the letter *q*, it always makes the same sound as *k*—so it transposes to the number 7.

The phonetic alphabet should become second nature to you. That is, whenever you hear or see the sound *r*, you should think, 4. When you hear or see 2, you should think, *n*. You must know them quickly and out of order. Go over them mentally now; you probably already know them. Those simple little memory aids make the phonetic alphabet easy to remember. Don't continue reading until you're familiar with the ten pairs of digits and sounds and have really practiced transposing sounds (*not* letters) to numbers.

Now. Without turning back to the first page of this chapter, do you remember the long-digit number that is at the top of that page? If you are like most people, the answer has got to be, "Are you kidding? Of course not."

But think: Do you remember the sentence that appears right under the long-digit number? Again, if you're among the majority, you do remember that sentence: "A beautiful naked blond jumps up and down." That's easy to picture, and if you simply thought of the picture when you first read the sentence, you'd have remembered it.

Well, look at that sentence, or think of it. What is the first consonant sound? The *b* in *b*eautiful. What digit does *b* represent? You should already know the answer—9. The next consonant sound is *t*; you know, by now, that *t* always represents the number 1.

Use paper and pencil and put down the digits for all the consonant sounds in that sentence. You already have 91. The word *beautiful* transposes to 9185. If you've transposed the entire sentence, you should have 91852719521639092112. Which *is* the number at the top of the first page of this chapter. And you thought you didn't remember it!

Have we made the point? It is much, much easier to remember the tangible sentence, which makes sense, than the intangible numbers. Had the sentence been "A pretty girl is like a melody," the number would have been 941745057351.

You *don't*, however, have to try to make the phonetic sounds of a long number form a sentence or cliché in order to remember the number—thanks to our old friend the Link.

Take this number:

941 140 494 275

The number has been broken into groups of three digits for teaching purposes only. Ordinarily you wouldn't break a number into equal groups like that. Try to think of a word that would phonetically fit 941. There are many such words; **parrot, bread, proud, apart, berate, pirate, brat, board, bored,** to name only a few. The first one you think of is usually the best for you to use.

Now look at the next group of three digits, 140. What word would fit those phonetically? **Tears, throws, throes, dress, duress** . . . Think of one yourself.

Now, start forming a Link; your association might be a

gigantic **parrot** wearing a **dress**. Be sure to see the picture. The next three digits are 494: **robber**, **rubber**, or **arbor** would fit phonetically. Continue your Link; you might picture a gigantic **dress** (just the dress; no lady in it) being a **robber**. See the picture; either the one suggested here or one you thought of yourself.

The last three digits are 275; **nickel**, **knuckle**, or **angle** would fit. Select one and continue your Link; associate robber (or whatever you used for 494) to nickel. You might see a gigantic **nickel** catching a **robber**, or being a robber.

You've just formed a short Link of only four words. But if you know those four words, if you know the Link, *you also know the twelve-digit number:* that is, if you also know the sounds.

Simply think of the first word of your Link, and transpose it to digits. If you used **parrot**, parrot can *only* break down to . . . 941. Think of parrot for a moment; that makes you think of—what? **Dress**, of course; and that can only transpose to . . . 140. Dress leads to **robber**, and robber transposes to . . . 494. And, finally, robber reminds you of **nickel**, and nickel can only be . . . 275. There are no decisions to make here; if you know the fundamentals—in this case, the sounds—any word breaks down, or transposes, to a specific group of digits.

Try it without looking at the book; see if you know the number. When you've tried it at least once, try it backward. Simply think of the last word of your Link; transpose it to digits and write, or say, those digits backward. That word will remind you of the next-to-last word, and so on. Nickel, robber, dress, parrot, *must* tell you—572494041149.

Do you see how applying both the Link and the phonetic alphabet has enabled you to memorize a long-digit number? What we've done is show you a way to turn abstract, intangible numbers into tangibles. Now you *can* picture numbers in your mind!

The only problem you may have had is transposing from sounds to numbers. If that slowed you down, it's because you don't know the sounds as well as you should—you haven't made them second nature. Obviously, the better you know the sounds, the faster you'll memorize numbers.

Let's try a longer one this time:

7412 3212 5390 0141 4952

Not at all impossible to remember—not now. Again, the number is broken into groups of four for teaching purposes only. Look at the first group; if you simply say the sounds to yourself, you'll almost automatically form a word. Say *k r t n;* you may have thought of **curtain, carton, cretin,** or **garden**—any one of which is perfect.

Look at 3212: *m n t n.* If you voice those sounds, you'll immediately think of something like **mountain** or **maintain.** If you picture a **carton** as large as a **mountain,** that's the start of your Link. Just be sure to see the picture. You needn't use our suggestions, of course; use whatever comes to mind—as long as the words fit the numbers phonetically, and your pictures are ridiculous.

Now, 5390: *l m p s.* You may have thought **lamps, limps,** or **lumps.** (No, **lambs** wouldn't do. That would transpose to 530; the *b* is silent.) Associate mountain to, say, lamps; you might see millions of **lamps** (it must be more than one lamp to remind you of the plural *s*) piled as high as a **mountain.** See that picture.

0141: *s t r t.* **Street, start,** or **store** it will do just fine. You might see many **lamps** walking down a **street,** or **starting** a race. See the picture.

4952: *r p l n.* You probably thought of **airplane,** and that's as good as any. Associate street or start to airplane; perhaps a gigantic **airplane** is parked on your **street.** Be sure to see the picture in your mind.

You've Linked only five words and those five words will remind you of a *twenty-digit* number. Try this on your own. Start with **carton** and go through your Link, to **airplane.** Transpose the consonant sounds into numbers as you go, and you'll see that you know the number!

Have you tried it? If you have, you should be pleased with yourself. Go a step further—try it backward. And, perhaps even more impressive, think of **parrot** and you'll see that you still remember the first (twelve-digit) number that we used as an example.

In a moment, we'll give you some numbers to practice with. But first: There's no rule that says that you must use a noun to represent any group of digits; nor must you use only one word for a group of digits—a phrase is just as good. In fact, there are some groups of digits that no single word would fit, but you can *always* find a phrase to fit. For example, we couldn't find a word for 989, but **puff up, pie fib,** or **beef pie** will serve the purpose. And although a phrase consists of two or more words, it's as easy to picture as one word.

Once you become familiar with the idea, you might look at 01414952, the last eight digits of the last example, and think **straight airplane.** That would have made the entire number easier and faster to memorize. Linking carton to mountain to lamps to straight airplane would have done it. And straight airplane (an airplane standing straight up on its tail) is one picture in your mind, although it consists of two words.

For a four-digit number like 4312, you might use raw **mutton, ram tin, roomed in, rhyme tone,** and so on. All can be pictured, and all fit phonetically. Even a particularly silly phrase, like **room die now,** can be pictured. Simply see a room dying now. If you thought of it, it can be pictured.

Don't lose sight of the basic idea. Aside from making numbers tangible, you're also forcing yourself to be Originally Aware of a number. Simply trying to come up with words or phrases *forces* you to concentrate on that number as you've never done before.

There are some standards that you can start using as you keep applying the idea. For example, whenever you see a zero, simply try to pluralize what comes before it. For 975, you might use **buckle**; if you see 9750, simply use **buckles**. For 27, always try to use the *-ing* ending; for 97527, use **buckling**. When you see a 4, you can try to use the *-er* ending; 9754 could be **buckler**. And for 1, you can use the past tense; 9751 would be **buckled**.

For 85, always try to use the *-ful* ending. The digits 92 might be **pain**, and 9285 would easily make you think of **painful**. Aside from these standards, you can use anything you like to remind you of any group of digits. Always use the first thing that comes to mind and fits phonetically, no matter how many digits it includes, and Link one thing to the other.

One more example:

943014918461087321984203l5

Here are only some of the ways to handle it: brooms, tripped over, jets, vacuum, knot, bufferins, metal. Pram, strip, tougher, jets off, come in, tip, frowns, my tail. Bear, master, pit, forage, toss off, commando, buffer, no summit, hill.

On your own, try your fantastic new memory for numbers on these:

839027195830274
10121650718430137
540381930136586926349
379205927153640
29384610452958573610265 4
619103481254027452

If you've really mastered the phonetic alphabet and practiced transposing, this formidable list isn't formidable for you. It's taken concentration, practice, and time to get to this point—well, we said at the outset that remembering numbers is the most difficult of memory chores. But again, think of the effort it would have taken (assuming you could have done it at all; few people could) to remember *one* long-digit number without a system.

It's true that most of you won't ever *need* to remember a twenty-digit number. Well, later we'll give you specific help with remembering the short-digit numbers you *do* need to know. But for now, you can enjoy the fact that anyone who can remember 91852719521639092112 is unlikely to forget, say, a telephone number.

If you *haven't* yet mastered the phonetic alphabet, you should take the time to really absorb those ten digit-sound pairs. Playing a mental game will help you do this faster: Whenever you see a number—an address, a license plate number, whatever—mentally transpose the digits into sounds. Whenever you see a word on a sign or billboard, transpose the consonant sounds to digits.

Do this for a while, and the sounds will become second nature. There are two traps to avoid: transposing according to letter instead of sound, and considering a double letter as two sounds instead of one. The *s* in the word *envision* transposes to 6, not 0; the *s* makes a soft *sh* sound. The same is true for the *t* in the word *position;* it transposes to 6, not 1. The word *pattern* transposes to 9142, not 91142—a double letter makes one sound only.

Play this mental game for a while; learn the sounds really well before you go on to the next chapter. Once the sounds have become second nature, you're ready for an amazingly useful memory system—the Peg.

THE PEG

HL: The student challenged me—he thought he could remember a long-digit number faster than I could. Another student wrote down the number and timed us. Well, I beat him by just a few seconds. (I wouldn't tell the story if he had beaten me!) In discussing it, we realized that we had used pretty near the same words and phrases for the numbers. We were both faced with 0384 at one point. He said that this was where he lost the few seconds, he couldn't think of a word or phrase quickly enough. He asked me what I had used, and I said, "Somevere." He said, "Somevere!? What kind of word is *that?*" Well, *somevere* wouldn't mean anything to anyone else but me. When I was growing up in a tenement on the Lower East Side of Manhattan, my neighbor was a sweet old man with a heavy accent. He always pronounced the word *somewhere* as *somevere.* This old gentleman was like a father to me, and left a lasting impression. So when I saw 0384, I thought of *somevere* and pictured him.

JL: It's a good story, but of course you could have used *samovar.*

HL: *Now* you tell me. And besides, I don't know what a samovar is.

•

Having memorized a list of items in sequence, using the Link, how would you know, say, the 8th item instantly? You wouldn't; you'd have to go over the Link and count, either mentally or on your fingers. There's a much easier way, using *Peg Words* that are based on the phonetic alphabet. This is the Peg system of memory.

If you know the sounds of the phonetic alphabet, and you should by now, this won't take much time or effort. We'll start by giving you ten Peg Words, then we'll show you how to use them.

Since the number 1 is always represented by the sound *t* or *d*, the Peg Word for 1 must contain only that sound. Many words could fit for any number, but the ones here are easy to picture and serve the purpose as well as any.

The word for 1 will always be **tie**. The word *tie* contains only one consonant sound, and that sound *(t)* can only represent 1. So, a mental picture of a man's necktie will always represent 1.

The number 2 is also a single digit, so the Peg Word must contain only one consonant sound—but now, that sound must be the sound that represents 2, which is *n*. The word (name) that will always represent 2 is **Noah**. Picture whatever you like, probably a man with a long gray beard, or just the beard.

The Peg Word for 3 will always be **Ma**; picture your mother, or a little old lady.

4: **rye**. That word could only represent 4 because it contains only one consonant sound, *r*. Picture a loaf of rye bread, or a bottle of rye whiskey.

5: **law**. Picture whatever law represents to you; we always picture a policeman.

6: **shoe**. Shoe contains only the *sh* consonant sound, which represents 6. Picture a shoe.

7: **cow**. Picture a cow, of course.

8: **ivy**. The *v* sound can only represent 8, therefore ivy can only represent 8. Picture ivy climbing on a wall.

9: **bee**. Picture the stinging insect.

The number 10 contains two digits, therefore the Peg Word for 10 must have the sound *t* (or *d*, for 1) and *s* (for 0) in that order. The word is **toes**; toes can only represent 10. Picture your toes.

Those are the first ten Peg Words. They are easy to remember because the phonetic sounds practically *tell* you what the words are. Look at them again; then see if you know them. You'll know them out of order because you know the *sounds* out of order. And they will never change; once you know them, they'll always be useful.

1.	tie	6.	shoe
2.	Noah	7.	cow
3.	Ma	8.	ivy
4.	rye	9.	bee
5.	law	10.	toes

Go over these a few times; you should be able to think of any number from 1 to 10 and know the Peg Word almost immediately. If you hear one of the Peg Words, you should, just as instantly, know the number it represents. When you know them fairly well, you're ready to learn how to use these Pegs.

Let's assume that you want to remember ten items in and out of order, by number. Let's also assume that you handle these items in a haphazard order.

You must remember that number 8 is **cracker**. There would, ordinarily, be no problem picturing a cracker, but how would you picture the 8? Well, it's easy if you learned the first ten Peg Words—the number 8 is . . . **ivy**. Simply associate cracker to ivy; see a ridiculous picture between those two items in your mind's eye, perhaps millions of crackers instead of ivy growing all over a brick wall.

Now. You want to remember that number 3 will be **scissors**. Associate scissors to your Peg Word for number 3, which is **Ma**. You might see yourself cutting your Ma in half with a gigantic pair of scissors. (That picture may make you shudder, but you won't forget it.) For each of these, be sure to *see* the picture you select; we won't bother reminding you again.

Number 5 will be **fish**. Associate fish to your Peg Word for the number 5, **law**. Perhaps a policeman is arresting a gigantic fish, or a large fish is walking the beat like a cop.

Number 1 is **pen**. You might see yourself wearing a gigantic pen, instead of a **tie** (your Peg Word for the number 1), around your neck—see the ink dripping all over your shirt.

Number 10 is **teeth**. Associate teeth to your Peg Word, **toes**. Perhaps you want to picture large teeth on your feet instead of toes, or teeth are biting off your toes.

Number 4 is **telephone**. Your Peg Word is **rye**; you might see yourself talking into a loaf of rye bread instead of a telephone, or a large bottle of rye whiskey is making a phone call.

Number 7 is **car**. Associate car to your Peg Word for the number 7, **cow**. See a cow driving a car, or you're milking a cow and cars come out instead of milk.

Number 2 is **article**. Your Peg Word for 2 is **Noah**; you must associate article to that. This is being used here purposely. If you want to picture millions of articles falling out of a long gray beard, fine. If you feel that article is too vague to picture, use a Substitute Word to remind you of it. You might use **ah tickle**, or a newspaper article. Use whatever you like, but be sure to associate it to beard, or whatever you're using to represent Noah.

Number 9 is **pillow**. Associate that to **bee**, your Peg Word for 9. Perhaps pillows, instead of bees, are swarming all over you and stinging you; or you're sleeping on a gigantic bee instead of a pillow.

Finally, you must remember that number 6 is **balloon**. The Peg Word for 6 is **shoe**. See yourself wearing balloons instead of shoes, or you're blowing up a shoe instead of a balloon. Use one of these, or one you thought of yourself, and see it in your mind's eye.

If you've made all the associations and visualized them clearly, there's no doubt that you know the ten items. Try it. Think of the Peg Word for number 1: tie. What does tie remind you of? What were you wearing instead of a tie? A pen, of course.

Think of Noah (2). That reminds you of . . . article.
Think of Ma (3). That reminds you of . . . scissors.
Think of rye (4). That reminds you of . . . telephone.
Think of law (5). That reminds you of . . . fish.
Think of shoe (6). That reminds you of . . . balloon.
Think of cow (7). That reminds you of . . . car.
Think of ivy (8). That reminds you of . . . cracker.
Think of bee (9). That reminds you of . . . pillow.
Think of toes (10). That reminds you of . . . teeth.

Aside from the fact that the items were given to you in an out-of-sequence order, you haven't really accomplished too much more than you could have accomplished with the Link. But there is a difference. If you want to know what number 6 is, simply think of the Peg Word for 6 (shoe) and you'll *instantly* know the 6th item! It's . . . balloon, right?

That's not all. If you think of any item, you'll instantly know its numerical position. Where was the telephone? Well, telephone makes you think rye, and rye is the Peg Word for the number 4, so telephone *has* to be 4.

If you'd like to test yourself, see how quickly you can fill in these blanks:

(cow) 7 = _____   (Ma) 3 = _____
(toes) 10 = _____   (bee) 9 = _____
(tie) 1 = _____   (law) 5 = _____
(shoe) 6 = _____   (Noah) 2 = _____
(ivy) 8 = _____   (rye) 4 = _____

And these:

    scissors is _____   balloon is _____
    telephone is _____   cracker is _____
    fish is _____   car is _____
    article is _____   teeth is _____
    pillow is _____   pen is _____

And these:

    10 is _____   car is _____
    3 is _____   fish is _____
    1 is _____   article is _____
    8 is _____   pillow is _____
    4 is _____   balloon is _____

Are you impressed with yourself? You should be. Having read them only once, you've remembered ten items forward, backward, and inside out.

The Peg Words are an extension of the places or "loci" idea mentioned at the beginning of the book. You've arrived at them slowly, step by step. The simple memory aids helped you to remember the sounds of the phonetic alphabet, the sounds themselves helped you to remember the Peg Words, and the Peg Words made it easy to remember ten random items. Obviously, the better you know the Pegs, the faster you'll be able to memorize a Peg list, as you just did.

But what if you have to remember eleven items, or twelve, or twenty? No problem. Knowing the phonetic alphabet enables you to make up Peg Words for any number. You can't picture the number 11, but you *can* picture a **tot**, a young child. And the word *tot* can only represent the number 11, because it has the *t* and *t* sounds, 1 and 1.

The Peg Word for 12 is **tin**; picture a tin can, or see the item at that position made of tin.

Then come:

13. **tomb**; picture a gravestone.	17. **tack**
14. **tire**	18. **dove**
15. **towel**	19. **tub**
16. **dish**	20. nose

Go over these once or twice and you'll know them. Now you can really show off. Have someone number a paper from 1 to 20 and let him call any number and any item, until each number has an item next to it. You make good strong associations, of course, of Peg Word to item. Next, call the items off from 1 to the last number. Then let your friend call any number—you tell him the item—followed by any item, whereupon you tell him the number!

A list of Peg Words up to 100 follows. They really are easy to learn, and there's no rote memory involved. Had the words been selected haphazardly, the idea would still work, but that would entail rote memory. As it is, the words all fit the pattern you've learned, and anything patternized is easier to remember. The sounds of the phonetic alphabet make it a fairly easy task.

We won't tell you that it's important for you to know them all thoroughly. You should know twenty or so perfectly, however, and we do suggest that you at least become familiar with all of them. Go over them, with concentration, a few times and you will be familiar with them. And, it can't hurt you in the least to really learn them all.

After you've gone over the words a few times, you can use this list as a drill. Put your hand or a piece of paper over the words, look at the numbers, and see if the word comes to you. If you like, you can make up flash cards, but that isn't really necessary. If you're stuck on a word, think of the consonant sounds, then stick vowels in there until the word comes to you. It will, sooner or later.

1. tie	26. notch	51. lot	76. cage
2. Noah	27. neck	52. lion	77. coke
3. Ma	28. knife	53. loom	78. cave
4. rye	29. knob	54. lure	79. cob
5. law	30. mouse	55. lily	80. fuzz
6. shoe	31. mat	56. leech	81. fit
7. cow	32. moon	57. log	82. phone
8. ivy	33. mummy	58. lava	83. foam
9. bee	34. mower	59. lip	84. fur
10. toes	35. mule	60. cheese	85. file
11. tot	36. match	61. sheet	86. fish
12. tin	37. mug	62. chain	87. fog
13. tomb	38. movie	63. chum	88. fife
14. tire	39. mop	64. cherry	89. fob
15. towel	40. rose	65. jail	90. bus
16. dish	41. rod	66. choo choo	91. bat
17. tack	42. rain	67. chalk	92. bone
18. dove	43. ram	68. chef	93. bum
19. tub	44. rower	69. ship	94. bear
20. nose	45. roll	70. case	95. bell
21. net	46. roach	71. cot	96. beach
22. nun	47. rock	72. coin	97. book
23. name	48. roof	73. comb	98. puff
24. Nero	49. rope	74. car	99. pipe
25. nail	50. lace	75. coal	100. disease

After you use the words for a while, you'll see that it's the picture that will come to mind when you see or hear a number, not the actual word. What happens when we see or hear, say, 36? We actually see a match, *not* the word *match*. This will happen automatically if you use the Peg Words—and you will use them, as you continue reading.

You'll learn many uses for the Peg Words. Going back to the long-digit numbers in the preceding chapter, for instance, when you're stuck on one or two digits in a number you can simply use the Peg Word and keep right on going. It saves time. Occasionally, you'll come to the end of a long number and still have one or two digits to take care of. Use the Peg Word for that.

And incidentally, if you see a group of like digits, don't worry—usually, like digits actually make a number easier to remember. Take 000000 in the middle of a long number—well, Souza's size would take care of five zeros; zoos sue Souza's sis would take care of eight zeros. You won't even have to do that if there are digits before and after the zeros—9000000941, passes (poses, possess) Souza's sport (or spirit) would do it.

If you're worried about the ridiculous pictures staying with you, running around in your mind forever, don't be. One of the beauties of the systems is the fact that all of them are means to an end. Once that end is accomplished, the means fade and disappear because they are no longer necessary. When the information is used a few times, you *know* that information—what you *won't* remember are your original silly pictures! That's one reason you can use the same Peg Words over and over again.

•

JL: The Peg Words are the handiest things—they've helped me get rid of some hostilities without anyone knowing what I'm talking about.

HL: Do you mean the names you sometimes yell out on the basketball floor?

JL: Right. When a referee makes what I think is an unfair call, and his number is thirty-three, I'll yell something like, "You, you— **mummy**!" Or if a player whose number is nineteen sticks an elbow in my ribs, I might call him "You **tub**, you!"—never mind some of the *other* names some numbers remind me of!

•

You've just learned the third of the three basic systems of memory: the Link, the Substitute Word, and now the Peg. We haven't been able to find any memory problem that could not be solved—made easier—by applying one of these three, or one in conjunction with another. It is sometimes necessary to twist or manipulate the systems somewhat, but they will still make any memory chore easier to handle.

Let's go back a bit. Earlier you learned to memorize the fifty states in alphabetical sequence; you also realized that you could associate a Substitute Word for the state to a Substitute Word for its capital city. To remember the states in sequence, you would use the Link system and the Substitute Word system. But now you can memorize them by number, in and out of order, by using the Substitute Word system and the Peg system.

You simply associate the Substitute Word or phrase for the state name to the vital Peg Word. Once you form a ridiculous picture in your mind between, say, **tie** and **album**, it will be easier to remember than to forget that the first (tie) state is Alabama (album), and vice versa.

Picture a con (prisoner) being a whiz (**whiz con**) with a **rope** (49), and you'll know that the 49th state, alphabetically, is Wisconsin. Picture yourself playing **tennis** (Tennessee) in the pouring **rain** (42), and you have the information you want.

A **new brass car** (Nebraska) is driving around and around your **neck** (27); millions of gigantic **pencils** (Pennsylvania) are seeing a **movie** (38); there are **peaches** (Georgia) growing between your **toes** (10); a **sassy can** (Kansas) is in a gigantic **dish** (16); a **nun** (22) is **mixing** something **again** and again (Michigan); a bride (**marry**) **lands** (Maryland) on your **nose** (20); a gigantic bottle of **gin**, wearing a **western** ten-gallon hat (West Virginia) is jumping off a **roof** (48); an **Indian** (Indiana) is wearing a **tire** (14) as a headdress; and so on.

Now you can remember not only nouns, but anything—by number. What works for the states can be applied to the Presidents of the United States. You might want to try to memorize them all by number, just for the mental exercise. It shouldn't take more than a few minutes. Find a list of the Presidents and apply the Substitute Word and Peg systems. (Here you'll be making up a Substitute Word for a person's name rather than for a place name—no difference, really.)

Some examples: The 11th President was Polk; you see yourself **pok**ing your finger through a **tot**; the 30th President was Coolidge, a **mouse** is **cool** on a building **ledge**; a (**blue**) **cannon** (Buchanan) is firing **towels** (15) instead of cannonballs; you're **pierc**ing (Pierce) a **tire** (14); a gigantic **tub** (19) is full of **hay**, or **haze** (Hayes); you pour ink on a door**knob** (29) and the **ink** gets **hard** (Harding); and so on.

The Peg and Substitute Word systems can be applied to concepts almost as easily. Suppose you had to learn the amendments to the Constitution of the United States, by number. Select one word, phrase, or thought from the amendment—the word, phrase, or thought that you think will remind you of the entire amendment. And usually, what *you* select *will* remind you of the entire concept. (This is the Key Word or Thought idea that we discussed in Chapter 6.) Now, associate that Key Thought to the Peg Word. That's all you have to do. It's really the same as what you did with states and Presidents, except that here the Substitute Word—the Key Thought—will remind you of much more information.

We're assuming that if you're interested in learning the amendments, or any material, you basically understand what it is you're studying. What you need are *reminders*.

For example, the seventh amendment to the Constitution gives the citizens of the United States the right to trial by jury. Associate cow (7) to that; all you really need to do is to see yourself in a courtroom, being judged by a **jury** of **cows**.

The fourth amendment has to do with protection against unreasonable search and seizure. See a gigantic loaf of **rye** bread (or a gigantic bottle of whiskey) coming into your **home** to **search** it; you can't stop him because he has a warrant to do so.

Picture a **tomb** being a **slave** driver to remind you that the thirteenth amendment abolished slavery.

The sixteenth amendment is the one we'd rather forget—the one that established the income tax. See yourself paying your **taxes** with **dish**es instead of money.

The eighteenth amendment started Prohibition—picture a **dove** trying to get into a **speakeasy**.

There is, of course, no way for us to use examples that will necessarily zero in on one of your specific, personal memory problems. What we're trying to accomplish is to make you aware of the variety of ways in which the systems can be applied. By the time you're finished with the book, you should have all the necessary weapons to face, attack, and solve any memory problem.

12

STYLE NUMBERS, PRICES, TELEPHONE NUMBERS

HL: I imagine the first thing most people who know that you memorized the first few hundred pages of the Manhattan telephone book wonder is, "Why on earth would anyone *want* to?"

JL: If they asked me, I'd tell them the truth—for the publicity. Actually, I memorized only the first column of every page. And the names and numbers don't start until page 22.

HL: That's still . . . let's see . . . maybe thirty thousand names and telephone numbers?

JL: At least. Anyway, I don't know them anymore. The stunt served its purpose—to publicize the systems that enable people to remember short numbers, like telephone numbers, instantly. And to keep on remembering them, as long as they want to.

•

The ability to picture numbers via the phonetic alphabet, plus the ability to use the Substitute Word system of memory is all that's necessary to help you remember style numbers, prices, and telephone numbers.

To remember a style number, associate the number to the product; it's that simple. If the style number of a typewriter is

691, associate **chopped** or **chipped** to typewriter. If you're in the typewriter business, then you'd have to associate the style number to the distinctive features of each machine, since you'd have many styles of typewriters. (Some style numbers include letters; you'll learn how to handle that, too.)

The same approach works for prices. Here are a few examples of different items and prices. Form the suggested ridiculous associations, or use your own, then you can test yourself and see if it works.

A lamp sells for $40.11; picture a **rested** or **roasted** lamp. See that picture.

A camera sells for $19.18; picture a gigantic camera being **tipped** off a table, or a camera **ta**king a picture of **taped** ivy.

Television set, $142.05; see a gigantic television set riding the tracks like a train; it has a sail on it (**train sail** = $142.05).

Toaster, $34.95; see a gigantic **marble** toasting bread, or a toaster popping up millions of marbles.

Car, $3,102.86; you might see a car taking a dose of **medicine** from a **fish**.

If you've tried to see these silly pictures, now try to fill in the correct prices:

toaster: $_____   television set: $_____

car: $_____   lamp: $_____

camera: $_____

When it comes to telephone numbers, there's no question that remembering them must save you a lot of time and aggravation over a long period. All you need do is calculate the minutes it takes to look up a number or dial the information operator, redial because you dialed the wrong number first, etc., to be convinced.

To remember a telephone number you simply associate a word or phrase that tells you the number (phonetically) to the person or company, or to a Substitute Word for the person or company. Eventually, the phone company will be using the ANC, All *N*umber Code, and there will be no exchange names. At the present time, some exchange names are still in use.

Remembering an all-digit phone number is the same as remembering any number. If your doctor's number is 940-8212, associate doctor (**stethoscope**, perhaps) to **press fountain**, or **brass fountain**, or **price fountain**. If you'd rather, you can associate the number to his name.

If you'd like to have your electrician's number at your fingertips, associate his number to **electric**. If the number is 862-9421, you might see an electric plug **fishin'** and drinking **brandy**, or you could use **fashion brand**. There's no rule that says your words must cover the first three digits and then the last four digits. Use any words to cover any of the digits; it doesn't matter. If a word that contains all the necessary sounds comes to mind —use it. For 720-5127, you might think of **cans looting**, which is fine, but **consulting** also would tell you the number.

As for exchange-name telephone numbers, there's a simple way to handle them. The first word in your association must tell you both the two exchange letters and the exchange number. You then use any word or phrase to tell you the remaining digits.

If the number you want to remember is RA 3-9110, the phrase **ram potatoes** would do it. The word *ram* begins with *ra*, and the very next consonant sound is *m*, for 3; RA 3. This becomes even easier when you realize that that first word needn't contain *only* the two letters and the one consonant sound. It must *begin* with that—then all following sounds are disregarded. So, you could have used **rampart potatoes** for this number, because **ram**part would still represent RA 3.

The word, or picture, **burn** would represent BU 4; **cigarette** would represent CI 7, **plan** or **plant** would represent PL 2, and so on. For exchanges like TN and LW (New York exchanges), with which it is impossible to form words, make up a standard. **Ton** could represent TN, and **low** could represent LW. For those, you'd know that a picture like **ton c**ow **marked** represents TN 7-3471. Later on, when you learn how to picture individual letters of the alphabet, you'll see how that would also help to solve this problem.

The publicity offices of Stein & Day, the publisher of this book, has the number PL 3-7285; we remembered it by associating a beer **stein** shining like the sun (**day**) to **plum can full**; the shining stein was pouring out enough plums to make a can full. Of course, we could have changed the exchange letters to digits, making the number 753-7285, and used **climb can full**, or **column can fall**.

This example brings us to two points. First, when you use two words for the last four digits, using the basic Peg Words, it may cause a slight confusion. If we had used **coin file**, how would we know, at a future time, that it was **coin file**, and not **file coin**? It doesn't matter that much—after you've dialed a number a few times, the picture you originally made isn't necessary anyway, you'll know the number. But, you can solve this minor problem by using any word *but* a basic Peg Word for the second word. If you make a habit of doing that, you'll know that the basic Peg Word always comes first. So, for the four digits 5230, you wouldn't use **lion mouse**, you'd use lion **mess, moss,** or **moose**.

The second point is that you can eliminate the necessity for forming words to cover the exchange name by eliminating the exchange name. You can look at a telephone dial and transpose the letters to digits, and the problem is solved. Since a telephone dial isn't always handy, the best thing to do would be to memorize it. Once you've done that, you can instantly transpose any exchange name or letters to digits.

Make up a word or phrase that reminds you of the three letters at each digit on a dial, and associate that to the digit (Peg Word). Here are some suggestions; really see the pictures, and you'll have memorized the dial in no time.

2—ABC: Picture **Noah** learning his **ABC**'s.

3—DEF: Picture your **Ma** being **deaf**.

4—**GHI**: See a **GI** drinking **rye,** or you're drinking **rye** and getting **high**.

5—JKL: Picture a **jackal** being a policeman (**law**).

6—MNO: Picture a **shoe** saying, "Me? **No**"; or a **shoe** being **mean** to an **O**.

7—PRS: See a **cow** carrying a gigantic **purse**.

8—TUV: Picture **ivy** being **tough** (enough to remind you of TUV).

9—WXY: A **bee** is **waxy**.

All that remain to be discussed are area codes. The area code simply changes a seven-digit phone number to a ten-digit number. Make up a word to represent the area code, put it into your original association, and you've got it. If Mr. Smith's telephone number is (201) 648-9470, you might see a picture of yourself smashing a **nest** (201) with a blacksmith's hammer; a **sheriff** (648) **breaks** (9470) your hammer.

Stein and Day's main offices are located in Westchester County (area code 914). The telephone number is 762-2151. A picture of a large slab of **butter** on a **cushion** that is **nettled** (or **not light**) would do it.

If you make many out-of-area calls, you might want to prememorize some area codes; just associate area code to place. Then you'll have them all ready when you need them. You can memorize the codes for major cities only, if you like. It's easy enough.

The area code for Manhattan is 212; that's almost ready-made for you because **Indian** represents 212 phonetically, and everyone knows that we bought Manhattan from the Indians. Or, you could associate **Indian** to **man hat**.

Associate **no time** to **lost angels** in order to remember that the area code for Los Angeles is 213.

The area code for all of Wyoming is 307; associate **Y roaming** to **mask**.

All of Delaware is 302; associate **Della wear** to mas**on**.

Nevada is 702; associate **never there** or **gambling** to **cousin**.

West Virginia is 304; associate a bottle of **gin**, wearing a western hat, to **misery** or **miser**.

Cleveland is 216; associate **cleave land** to **no touch**.

Chicago is 312; associate **chick** (**car go**) to my **tan**, **median**, or **mutton**.

Again, you'll need the silly pictures only until the numbers become knowledge. Best of all, you'll have liberated yourself from misdialed calls, telephone books, and telephone operators!

13 PLAYING CARDS

JL: I've seen you handle a deck of cards—I don't blame casinos for not wanting to deal blackjack to you.

HL: There are six who won't, that I know of. But, they're not being as smart as they think. Sure, I'll probably beat the house at blackjack, but then I lose that and more at the crap tables.

JL: Memory systems won't help you *there*.

HL: No, but a combination of memory systems and knowledge of the game really works for blackjack. It's actually the only casino game where you can better the odds, sometimes even the odds, or change them so that you have a bit of an edge.

JL: Is that because you can double your bet after the hand has started?

HL: Right. And remembering exactly which cards have been played is a great help in knowing when to double your bet, and when to stop or hit. I have to tell you, it's not so easy nowadays. Thanks to people who know our systems, most casinos use more than one deck—and never deal down to the end.

JL: Too bad, **Harry**, you'll have to work for your money!

•

Playing cards are difficult to remember because they are abstractions; they're like numbers. There's really no way most people can picture a card, so again the concept here is to make an intangible tangible. The trick is to have each card of a deck represented by a definite, concrete item—just as you did with numbers. Once that's accomplished you'll be able to picture playing cards, and then they can be associated to other things just as numbers can. There's a different, very easy way to remember cards—the "missing card" or "mutilation" idea —which we'll get to shortly.

Incidentally, you should learn the ideas in this section whether or not you play cards. You never know, you may become interested in cards in the future—but more important, trying the ideas is a great mental exercise.

The pattern used is almost obvious. The Card Word for each card (up to the 10's) will begin with either C, H, S, or D—for clubs, hearts, spades, and diamonds. The very next consonant sound in that word will be the sound that represents the *value* of the card. So, the word **can** could represent only the 2C. That's the pattern, and once you understand it, there are no decisions or choices to make. **Can** represents the 2C because it begins with a C for *c*lubs, and the next consonant sound is *n*, for 2.

The word (or picture) **sail** must represent the 5S, because it begins with an *s* (for spades) and is followed by the *l* sound, for 5. The 4H is **hare**; 6D is **dash**; 4C is **core**; 8S is **safe**; 9D is **deb**; AD is **date** (ace is 1); 6C is **cash**; and so on.

Be sure you fully understand these few examples before you continue reading. Then look at the Card Words on page 137. As you look them all over, you'll see that the jacks, queens, and kings represent a departure from the pattern, which we'll explain momentarily.

The *s* sound is used to represent the 10's. Since there is no zero of any suit, we might as well use that sound for the 10's. So, the pattern or system holds for all the cards from ace to 10.

Don't worry about the *ds* in suds, for the 10S. It's really one

AC—cat	AH—hat	AS—suit	AD—date
2C—can	2H—hen	2S—sun	2D—dune
3C—comb	3H—hem	3S—sum	3D—dam
4C—core	4H—hare	4S—sewer	4D—door
5C—coal	5H—hail	5S—sail	5D—doll
6C—cash	6H—hash	6S—sash	6D—dash
7C—cake	7H—hog	7S—sock	7D—dock
8C—cuff	8H—hoof	8S—safe	8D—dive
9C—cup	9H—hoop	9S—soap	9D—deb
10C—case	10H—hose	10S—suds	10D—dose
JC—club	JH—heart	JS—spade	JD—diamond
QC—cream	QH—queen	QS—steam	QD—dream
KC—king	KH—hinge	KS—sing	KD—drink

sound—*dz*, which represents 0. And even if you break it into two sounds, that's *d-s*, which is 1-0. It can represent only 10.

Besides, the words up through the 10's fit the pattern and can be pictured, the court card words also can be pictured—so the word itself isn't that important. It's the picture the word creates in your mind that matters—after some use, you shouldn't think the word but simply see the picture it creates.

Once you've seen a picture in your mind for any word, that's the picture you should (and will) see each time. A few suggestions: For core, picture an apple core; for cuff, trousers; case, either a briefcase or a crate; hem, a dress; hash, corned-beef hash; hoof, a horseshoe; hoop, a basketball hoop; hose, nylons or a garden hose; suit, a man's suit jacket (this is to distinguish it from cuff); sum, an adding machine or a sheet of paper covered with numbers; sash, a window sash or just a window; suds, a tub full of sudsy water; date, the fruit or a calendar; dune, a sand hill; dam, Boulder Dam or a waterfall; dash, a track star running the 100-yard dash; dock, a pier; deb, a debutante; dose, a spoonful of medicine—we simply picture a spoon.

For the picture, or court, cards we could have stayed within the pattern, but it gets a little sticky to come up with words like **hated** for the JH (since jack is 11, queen is 12, and king is 13), and **cotton** for the QC. It can be done, and we'll give you a list of words that stay with the pattern, so don't decide yet which method you'll use for the court cards.

We prefer to use the Card Words as listed. For the jacks, simply use the suit words themselves; they each have meaning —a club, a heart (the organ, or a Valentine card), a spade (shovel), and a diamond. For the QH and KC, we use the words queen and king, respectively. Just be sure that you differentiate between the two pictures since they're similar, both royalty. For queen, picture a lady wearing a crown and a *gown* on a throne; for king, picture the crown but be sure he's wearing *trousers*.

The words for the remaining queens and kings each begin with the vital suit letter, but then each word *rhymes* as closely as possible to queen and king. They're not exact rhymes (except for **sing**), but close enough. Don't worry about these; you'll probably remember them easily because they *are* exceptions. For steam, picture a radiator; for dream, a bed or someone sleeping.

As was the case with Peg Words, if you go over the Card Words a few times you may be surprised at how quickly you'll know them.

Now. As promised, here are the words for the court cards that stay within the pattern. You have choices for all of them, and you'll have to decide whether you want to use these or the ones we use. Again, it doesn't really matter. We had to use phrases for three of the kings, and take a bit of license with the JH and QH, but they will work just as well because they do create a picture in the mind.

JC—cadet, coated
JH—hothead, hated, hooted,
       hooded

JS—steed, staid, sated
JD—dotted, doted, dead
       head, dead heat, dated
QC—cotton, codeine
QH—hootin', heatin',
       hatin', headin', Hayden
       (Planetarium), hoe down
QS—satan, satin, sit in,
       sadden, sedan
QD—detain, deaden, dotin'
KC—cute Ma, caddie me
KH—head home, high dome,
       hit me, high time, hide me
KS—steam, stem
KD—dead aim, tea time (the
       t will still remind you of
       d for diamond)

Make your decision as to which method to use for the court cards, and then put in a little time learning all the words or phrases. You'll find the Card Words just as effective an aid for remembering playing cards as the Peg Words are for remembering numbers. Obviously, they can't be much help until you know them fairly well. As was true of the Peg Words, any words would serve the purpose. But because these are patternized, you eliminate rote memory. If you know the pattern and the phonetic sounds, the chore is half done.

If you like, you can easily make up a deck of flash cards. Simply write the correct Card Word on the back of each card. Shuffle them and look at them one at a time—either back or face. If you see the face, call out the Card Word, then turn the card over to see if you're right. If you see the back, the Card Word, call out the name of the card and turn it over to check. When you get to the point where you can do this with all fifty-two cards, *without hesitation*, you know the Card Words fairly well.

All right, assuming you know the Card Words, how do you apply them? Well, now you can remember cards as easily as you remember items. You can use the Link to remember cards in sequence. A Link of a gigantic apple **core** taking a **drink**, a **doll** drinking, a gigantic **cake** rocking a doll in its arms, a cake acting as the **sail** of a sailboat, a sail(boat) shining in the sky like the **sun**, the sun having long ears and hopping about like a **hare**, a gigantic **cup** hopping like a hare, a large cup wearing **socks**, and a gigantic sock being a radiator (**steam**), would help you remember the 4C, KD, 5D, 7C, 5S, 2S, 4H, 9C, 7S, and QS—in sequence, forward and backward.

Or you can use the Peg system to remember cards by number, in and out of order. This is quite an impressive memory demonstration, because you are memorizing two abstracts, numbers and cards. You need to know two things—the Peg Words from 1 to 52, and the Card Words. You can do it with a full deck; but it's just as impressive with half the deck, or even twenty cards.

Just to show you how it works, assume a friend shuffles the cards and calls off ten of them, from the top. Make these associations or use your own pictures:

You're wearing a large horseshoe (**hoof**) instead of a **tie**.

A man's beard (**Noah**) is made up of millions of dollar bills (**cash**).

Your **Ma** is **singing** at the Metropolitan Opera.

A **hen** is laying a bottle of **rye** instead of an egg, or it's drinking from a bottle of rye.

A gigantic **comb** is wearing a uniform; it's a policeman (**law**).

A gigantic **shoe** is sitting on a throne, wearing royal robes; it's the **king**.

It's **hailing cows** instead of hailstones.

Millions of **cups**, instead of **ivy**, are growing all over a wall; or, ivy is growing all over a gigantic cup.

You open a **safe**, and millions of **bees** fly out and sting you.

You're wearing **toes** instead of a **hat**; or hats are growing between your toes.

If you've really tried to see these or your own pictures, and if you're fairly familiar with the Card Words, you'll know ten cards by number. It's quite easy. Think of the Peg Word for number 1, **tie**. What does it make you think of? It should make you think of horseshoe, or hoof. **Hoof** can represent only one card, and that's the 8H.

Try it on your own; think of each of the Peg Words up to 10. Each one should make you think of a Card Word. Transpose that to a card, and you'll have remembered the card at that position. See if you can fill in these blanks:

Card 2 (Noah)   is the _____.
Card 3 (Ma)   is the _____.
Card 4 (rye)   is the _____.
Card 5 (law)   is the _____.
Card 6 (shoe) is the _____.
Card 7 (cow)   is the _____.
Card 8 (ivy)   is the _____.
Card 9 (bee)   is the _____.
Card 10 (toes) is the _____.

Since this is exactly the same as doing a regular Peg list, you also know the cards out of order. If you thought of **cow** (7), the picture of hailing cows should come to mind, and **hail** can only be the 5H. If your friend called the KS, you'd transpose that to its Card Word, **sing**, which should make you think of **Ma**, and that tells you that the KS is the third card. Test yourself—number or card. If you made the associations originally, you'll know the position of each card, and which card is at which position. If you didn't form the associations, go back and do so now. Otherwise, you'll never know whether or not this really works!

Knowing the Card Words makes the cards of a deck tangible and easy to picture in the mind. Once they can be pictured, they can be associated so that you can be Originally Aware of them.

Here's some more practice for you, although you can easily do it on your own. Use the Peg Words from 11 to 20 and remember the following cards. Then you'll know twenty cards by number. After you've formed the associations, test yourself.

11. 4D (tot to door)
12. JS (tin to spade)
13. 3H (tomb to hem)
14. 8D (tire to dive)
15. 10C (towel to case)
16. 6S (dish to sash)
17. 10H (tack to hose)
18. 7H (dove to hog)
19. 5D (tub to doll)
20. KH (nose to hinge)

Now that you've impressed yourself, you're ready to learn a fascinating application of the Card Words.

Neither the Link nor the Peg would come in too handy in most card games. For any "discard" game such as gin rummy, bridge, hearts, or canasta, you need the "mutilation" idea. We'll teach it to you as a stunt, and then we'll discuss its use in different card games.

Assume that a friend shuffles a full deck of cards. He removes, say, five cards, which he puts into his pocket without looking at them. Now, he calls off the remaining forty-seven cards. When he's done that, you tell him, one by one, the cards he has in his pocket—in other words, you tell him the names of the *missing* cards.

There's no need to use the Link or the Peg in order to

accomplish this; it would take much too long. The mutilation idea is faster and easier because all you need to know is your list of Card Words. You simply do this: When you hear a card called, transpose it to its Card Word and *mutilate* that word (the picture, really) in some way.

Say the KD is called, see a *spilled* drink; the 4H is called, picture a hare *without* ears; the 5D, see a doll with an arm or leg missing; the AC, see a cat without a tail; the 2S, see a cloud obliterating the sun, and so on. Simply mutilate the picture that represents the card in your mind, in some quick way. This will become easier and faster to do as you keep doing it, for two reasons: You'll get to know the Card Words better, and once you see a mutilation of any Card Word, you'll use that same picture all the time. It has become an instantaneous picture in your mind.

This is probably the best example of pinpointed concentration and Original Awareness that we could demonstrate. That instantaneous picture of the mutilated Card Word has forced you to be aware of that particular card at that moment, as clearly as is humanly possible. You can prove this by trying it. After you've mutilated the called forty-seven cards, all you have to do is to go over all your Card Words, mentally. Any Card Word that has *not* been mutilated will stand out like the proverbial sore thumb!

Go over the Card Words in a specific order; we always use CHSD, which is easy to remember if you think of the word "chased." Perhaps you'd prefer the HSDC order—think of the phrase "his deck." You might want to use the bridge, or alphabetical, order of suits (CDHS), it doesn't matter. Always using the same suit order will save you the time and possible confusion of possibly going over the same suit twice. Why take the chance of going over, say, the club Card Words, calling the one or two club cards that are in your friend's pocket, then the hearts—and then not being sure which suits you've already done?

Going over the suits in the same order every time eliminates that possibility.

It doesn't matter how many cards you tell your friend to take from the deck. Actually, the more cards he removes, the easier it is for you; there'll be fewer cards for you to mutilate. Five cards is a good demonstration for poker players; for gin rummy players, have someone remove ten cards. For a bridge demonstration, you can have someone shuffle and then deal out the four hands of thirteen cards each. He then takes three of the hands, shuffles, and calls them off to you a card at a time. You should be able to name all thirteen cards in the fourth hand.

To gain speed, you should first work at making the Card Words second nature; the better you know them, the faster you'll be able to do the missing-card demonstration. After you've tried it a few times at a rate and speed you find comfortable, push yourself a bit—have a friend call the cards to you at a little faster pace than you think you can handle. Tell your friend not to slow down or stop for any reason. Then you have no choice but to "see" each mutilation within that particular slot of time. We think you'll find, believe it or not, that not only will you do the stunt (you'll know the missing cards), but you'll do it *better*.

You'll be forcing yourself to see each picture quickly and clearly, and that's better than trying to think of or see each picture for too long a period. The next time, try it at an even faster pace, and so on. If you own a metronome, set it at the pace you desire and turn a card face up whenever that pendulum swings to one side.

If you haven't as yet, you should try the missing-card stunt before you continue. Take some cards out of a shuffled deck, then look through the others—mutilating as you do. Then go over the Card Words mentally and jot down the cards you think are not mutilated, or missing. Check to see if you're correct. If you want to save a little time, remove the picture cards, then you'll be working with only forty cards. After you've mutilated, you're left with only the Card Words from aces to 10's to go over.

You may be wondering how you can repeat the missing-card demonstration. Well, you *shouldn't* repeat it immediately for the same people. Once is enough; leave them wanting more. You can repeat it, however, if you want to. If you use mutilation again, of course, it would be confusing. This brings us to playing, say, gin rummy. Obviously, if you're applying the missing-card principle, you're going to have to do it with each hand played.

All right; for the first hand, use mutilation; for the next hand, use fire. That is, see each Card Word *burning*. It's a form of mutilation, but different enough so as not to cause confusion. For the next hand, use *water;* see each Card Word under water, or drowning. For the next hand, see each Card Word being cut with a *knife,* and for the next hand, associate each Card Word to *yourself.* The idea is to force yourself to concentrate on each card for that one fraction of a second, and each of the above-mentioned methods will serve—yet they're all different, and definite, enough to be distinct in your mind. You need only try it to see that this is so.

By the time you've reached the associating-to-yourself method, you're ready to go back to mutilation and start the entire cycle over again. You can, however, enlarge the cycle if you like. After associating the Card Words to yourself, for the next hand of gin you can associate each Card Word to the Peg Word for 1 (tie), next hand to Noah, next to Ma, and so on. By then, you'll surely be able to start the cycle over again without confusion.

In gin rummy, it is important to know whether or not it is safe to discard any particular card. As you play, mutilate—or burn, or whatever—each card discarded by yourself and your opponent. When you want to be sure that a card is safe, you don't have to go through all your Card Words—that would take too long. All you need do is think of three or four Card Words.

Say you're about to discard the 8H. Is it safe? Think of the Card Words for the 7H and the 9H. If they haven't been mutilated, don't throw that 8H—your opponent may be holding a heart run, and waiting for the 8H. If the surrounding cards (7H and 9H) have been mutilated, don't throw the 8H yet; think of the Card Words for two other 8-spots. If they've been mutilated, you *know* it's safe to discard the 8H.

If and when your opponent takes a discard, associate the Card Word to his, say, nose. He takes the 7S; see a **sock** hanging from his nose. Later, when you need to know what cards he took from the discard pile, you'll know the cards! Associating the Card Word to him in some silly way makes you Originally Aware of the card. You can do this during each hand, without getting confused. Try it and see for yourself.

Bridge players use this idea to great advantage. Exactly how is up to the particular player. Some are interested in knowing only the trump cards that have been played, so they mutilate only trump cards. More experienced players may want to know all the cards that are played, so they mutilate each one as it falls. Once you understand the idea, apply it as you desire, and to your best advantage.

For pinochle, which is played with a deck of forty-eight cards containing only 9's through aces, you need two Card Words for each card from the 9's on. One fast example: For the 9C, you'd use the basic Card Word (**cup**) and perhaps **cap** for the second 9C; the pattern is the same. When playing, you'd mutilate **cup** when the first 9C is played, and **cap** when the second one is played. Always mutilate the basic Card Word first, then the one you made up for the second like card. For the court cards, use a word (for the second card) that the basic Card Word reminds you of. For example, **drink** might remind you of **glass**, so you can use glass to represent the second KD.

Poker is not a discard game, but a memory of what's been

played is certainly helpful in most games. Good poker players do know poker odds—the chances of drawing to an inside straight, or whatever. And those odds do change according to cards played. So in an open, or stud, poker game it would be foolish to keep betting because you're waiting for a 9-spot, when you know (remember) that two 9's have already been dealt to other players. Players drop out and turn their cards down—a good player will remember the cards that he's seen during the hand, and play accordingly.

Even in a game like five-card draw, where you see none of the cards, our memory systems can help you to remember the odds for bettering your hand. For example, if you have three cards of the same suit and you want to know whether or not it pays to stay in and draw for two more of the same suit (a flush), remembering that the odds are approximately 23 to 1 against drawing that flush may help you to decide not to do it!

The word **flame**, under these circumstances, would remind you of flush-three cards. The first two letters of the word (*fl*) remind you of flush, and the next consonant sound reminds you of three cards. Associate **flame** to **name** (23), and you have your reminder. The odds against drawing one card (you retain four) to a flush are approximately 5 to 1. Associating **flare** (flush, while retaining four) to **law** (5) will do it.

Many poker players will stay in the game holding a pair and a "kicker," then drawing two cards. It might help you to know that the odds against making three-of-a-kind that way are 12 to 1. Picture a sheet of **tin** (12) **kicking** a **pear**, and you'll be able to remember this easily. The odds against making two pair under these circumstances are 5 to 1; a **pear** kicking a **policeman** (**law**) will do it. Your knowledge of the game will tell you whether the odds pertain to three-of-a-kind or two pair; or, you can put another word into the association to tell you what it pertains to.

In bridge, the chances of drawing thirteen cards of any one suit are 1 in to **love, climb, move up, poses**! The chances of drawing thirteen spades are 1 in show **mule, steam, lily up, chases!** And in poker, the odds against drawing one of the four possible royal flushes are **sharp camp** to 1. Don't bet on any of these!

The odds against rolling an eleven in one roll of the dice are 17 to 1. That's why the house has the edge at the crap table when they offer 10 or 15 to 1 on eleven.

Of course, no amount of memory of odds, or cards played, will help you much if you don't really know the strategy of the game that you're playing. We don't want to mislead you into thinking that having a great memory will make you a winner; it won't unless you're a good player. We relinquish all responsibility for your losses—but you can send us 10 percent of your winnings!

WEEKLY APPOINTMENTS; DAYS OF THE WEEK

HL: Remembering the time and place of appointments is obviously important, both in business and socially.

JL: Of course, you can remember the right place and time, and still get fouled up. In Boston, one player made a date with a girl and he was to meet her outside her hotel, after the game. It was *two degrees below zero* that night.

Some of us were going to a restaurant after the game, and we saw him waiting there. When we finished eating, we went back to the hotel, and he was still standing there! As we passed him, he asked, "Is this the front or the back of the hotel?"

●

In an earlier chapter, you learned that a Link would help you remember simple errands and appointments for the following day. That idea alone will suffice for many people. However, you may have to remember more specific appointments, by day and time, and for the following week.

It's easy enough to do; you already have the necessary knowledge. The problem is familiar to you—how do you picture a day and time? The solution is just as familiar. Set up a pattern that enables you to create a picture for any day and time; to make the intangible tangible.

In patternizing day and time, we'll consider Monday the first day of the week. Since it is the first business day of the week, this makes more sense to most people. If you'd rather consider Sunday the first day, simply do so and change everything accordingly; it won't matter once you understand the idea. Otherwise, go along with us. Monday is the first day, Tuesday is second, and so on to Sunday, the seventh day of the week.

Thursday at 7:00 can now be thought of as a two-digit number. Thursday is the fourth day, so the first digit is 4, to represent the day. The second digit represents the hour —therefore, the two-digit number is 47. Within this pattern, 47 can represent only the fourth day (Thursday), seventh hour (7:00).

Ordinarily, it would be just as difficult to picture 47 as it would be to picture Thursday at 7:00. But you have a Peg Word for 47 that can be pictured—**rock**. And so, within this pattern, **rock** must represent Thursday at 7:00.

The Peg Word **knife** could represent only Tuesday (second day) at 8:00. **Lily** must represent the fifth day (Friday) at 5:00. Even if you don't know the Peg Words, the sounds give you the necessary information. This will work much more smoothly, of course, if you *do* know the Peg Words. Try a few yourself— mentally transpose these Peg Words to day and hour: **name, chain, knob, net, dish, Nero, coal, mower.**

There are a few minor problems remaining. How do you handle 10:00, 11:00, and 12:00? What about A.M. and P.M.? What about minutes? And, how do you *use* the Peg Words?

Let's take care of 10:00, 11:00, and 12:00 first. Remember our discussion of playing cards—just as there is no zero of hearts, there is also no zero o'clock. So, use the *s* sound to represent 10:00. **Mouse** will represent Wednesday at 10:00; **toes**, Monday at 10:00; **rose**, Thursday at 10:00; **nose**, Tuesday at 10:00; **case**, Sunday at 10:00; and so on.

It is necessary to make up a word for each day of the week at

11:00 and 12:00. There are two ways to handle this: the first is to stick with the pattern and use a word containing the proper sounds. The word **mitten**, for example, is Wednesday at 12:00 (312); and **rotate** (411) could represent only Thursday at 11:00.

Here is a list of words from which you can select. Make up your own, if you'd rather.

1) Monday:
   11:00—dotted, toted

   12:00—titan, tighten, deaden

2) Tuesday:
   11:00—knotted, knitted, noted

   12:00—Indian, antenna

3) Wednesday:
   11:00—mated, imitate, matted

   12:00—mitten, maiden, mutton

4) Thursday:
   11:00—rotate, raided, ratted

   12:00—rotten, written, rattan

5) Friday:
   11:00—lighted, loaded

   12:00—laden, Aladdin

6) Saturday:
   11:00—cheated, jaded, jotted

   12:00—jitney, shut in, chutney

7) Sunday:
   11:00—coated, cadet
   12:00—kitten, cotton

Select the words you want, and use them. After a few uses, they will be like Peg Words—for this pattern. You'll know them *because* you've used them.

Here's another way to handle 11:00 and 12:00: Simply consider 11:00 and 12:00 as 1:00 and 2:00, but without using the basic Peg Words since you're already using them. Use any *other* word that fits phonetically.

For example, the Peg Word **mat** represents Wednesday at 1:00, but the words **meat** or **moat** could represent Wednesday at 11:00. The Peg Word **moon** represents Wednesday at 2:00—use

man or **moan** to represent Wednesday at 12:00. Once you select the words, they will work perfectly well. You'll know that the basic Peg Words represent 1:00 and 2:00, and that any other words that fit 1:00 and 2:00 (for any day) would represent 11:00 and 12:00.

If all your appointments were made on the hour, you'd be all set to apply the system—by associating the appointment itself to the word that represents the day and hour of the appointment. If you had to go to the library on Saturday at 1:00, you'd form a ridiculous association between library, or books, and **sheet**. That's all.

Why not make that association now? Then we'll list some more, just to show you how it works. Later, we'll get to the minutes, and to A.M. and P.M. These hypothetical appointments will be given to you haphazardly, since that's how appointments usually come up. Form the associations, because we're going to test you.

On *Tuesday at 9:00*, you have a dental appointment. Transpose the day and hour to the Peg Word, **knob**, and associate that to dentist. Perhaps the dentist is pulling a doorknob instead of a tooth out of your mouth. Or a gigantic doorknob is your dentist. Be sure to see the picture.

Monday at 2:00, you have a meeting at the bank. Associate **tin** (first day, second hour) to bank. Perhaps you're depositing sheets of tin instead of money; or the bank tellers are all large tin cans.

Saturday at 8:00, you must remember to leave your car at your garage for repairs. Associate **chef** to car. You might see a gigantic chef's hat driving a car, or a car is wearing the chef's hat.

Wednesday at 5:00, you have to pick up a pair of eyeglasses. Associate **mule** to glasses. The silly picture of a mule wearing gigantic eyeglasses would do it. See that picture.

Friday at 2:00, you have a luncheon appointment with Mr.

Vaikovitch. Associate **lion** to, perhaps, **vague witch**. See a lion about to eat a witch, only the witch starts to fade; it gets vague. Or, a lion is trying to **wake** a **witch**.

Thursday at 10:00, you want to remember your karate lesson. Associate **rose** to karate. Perhaps you're giving a gigantic rose a karate chop, or a gigantic rose is using karate on you.

Tuesday at 5:00, there's a meeting of the volunteer fire department. Associate **nail** to fire. Perhaps a gigantic nail is starting a fire. Be sure to see this picture.

Now try this. Go over your Peg Words for Monday—**tot, tin, tomb,** up to **toes.** (If you still don't know the Peg Words, turn back to the list and read them. Picture each one as you read.) Now, when you come to a word that has been associated to something else, you'll know it instantly! You've only got to try it to see that this is so. Just now, when you thought **tin,** that should have made you think of . . . bank.

After you've done Monday, go over Tuesday's words—**net, nun, name,** etc. Then Wednesday's, Thursday's, Friday's, Saturday's, and Sunday's. Think of the words up to zero (10:00) only, since there are no 11:00 and 12:00 appointments used in the example. If you do this, you'll probably remember all the appointments!

Just exactly how would you apply this idea? Well, assume it's the following Monday. In the morning, go over Monday's Peg Words; there are only twelve. You'll be reminded of the things you must do that day. During the day, while you're having lunch, walking, etc., simply go over those words. You'll have a constant reminder of your appointments. If you'd rather know what it is you have to do the *next* day, go over Monday's words on Sunday night. That's all there is to it. No more looking for your appointment book, which you probably left at home or at the office anyway.

For the minutes, simply add one word to the Peg Word picture. If you have a plane to catch on Friday at 5:20, **lily** is the

Peg Word that represents Friday at 5:00. You could make 5:20 **lily nose**—**nose** tells you the minutes. There's one problem here; next week, how would you know whether it's lily nose or nose lily? (If you thought it was nose lily, you'd go to the airport three days too soon!)

The problem is easily solved by *not* using a basic Peg Word to represent minutes—use any other word that fits phonetically (just as with the idea for 11:00 and 12:00). For the above example, use **noose** or **niece**. A ridiculous picture of a gigantic lily with a noose around its neck, flying like an airplane, would do it. This solves the problem because you'd know that the basic Peg Word always represents day and hour, and any other word always represents the minutes.

Frankly, we rarely use the minute idea. Our appointments are almost never that precise. All we really need is a reminder for a quarter, a half, and three-quarters past the hour. We use a standard to represent each one. A twenty-five-cent piece always represents a **quarter** past the hour, a **half** grapefruit represents half past the hour, and a pie with one large slice gone (**three-quarters** of a pie) represents three-quarters past the hour. Use these standards, or make up your own.

The standards work for us, because even if we want to remember, say, a 6:19 appointment (an airplane departure or a television taping), we'll consider it as 6:15. The worst (or best) that can happen is that we're a little early for the appointment. If the appointment is for 2:38, we consider it as 2:30.

The A.M.-P.M. question is really a hypothetical one. You usually know whether any particular appointment is A.M. or P.M. If you really had a luncheon appointment with Mr. Vaikovitch at 2:00, you'd hardly assume it was 2:00 A.M.! You'd also know that your 9:00 dental appointment is in the morning, unless you have a very unusual dentist.

You can, however, make the association as definite as you want to. You can use **aim** to represent A.M. Or, you can use **white** to represent day (A.M.), and **black** to represent night (P.M.). All you really need is one of them. To remember that an appointment is in the morning, get white into the picture; if white isn't in the picture, then you know it's a P.M. appointment.

In the example of bringing your car to the garage on Saturday at 8:00, you could have pictured the car being sparkling white, or **aiming** at something, to remind you that the appointment was at 8:00 A.M.

•

JL: Harry, the truth now—did you ever miss an engagement because you forgot about it, and just didn't show up? I've heard something to that effect.

HL: It makes a good story, but no. Years ago, I was scheduled to appear at a Rotary Club luncheon, and I had quite a drive to get there. Somebody told me that it was a two-hour drive, and it ended up a four-hour drive. When I got there, all the Rotarians had left. There was quite a story in the next day's local paper, headed, MEMORY EXPERT FORGETS TO SHOW UP!

JL: That sounds as if it might really have happened.

HL: It did. Anyway, you shouldn't bring up things like that. If you keep it up, I'll have to tell people about the time you were driving through the exact-change booth at a tunnel, threw the half-dollar, and missed the bucket!

•

In the next chapter, we'll discuss how to remember monthly appointments, birthdays and anniversaries, and historical dates. We'll even touch on a bit of astrology. But first, an idea that may make you wonder why you didn't think of it yourself.

Suppose someone you're talking to says, "I'll be away during most of March, why don't we have lunch on April ninth?" (We're using the year 1974 in these examples.) And *you* immediately say, "Sorry, that's a Tuesday, and I play golf on Tuesdays." How did you know that April 9 falls on a Tuesday?

Well, here's a method you can use to figure, almost instantly, the day of the week for any date within the current year.

Look at this twelve-digit number: 633 752 741 631. If you memorize that number, you'll be able to know the day of the week for any date in 1974. How? It's simple; those twelve digits give you the first Sunday of the month for each of the twelve months. The first Sunday in January, 1974, is the 6th of the month; the first Sunday in February is the 3rd; the first Sunday in March is the 3rd; the first Sunday in April is the 7th; and so on to December, the first Sunday of which is the 1st of the month.

By now, you should have no trouble memorizing a twelve-digit number. You might Link **shame him** to **clown** to **cart** to **jammed**, or whatever words or phrases you come up with.

Once you've memorized the number, knowing the first Sunday of the month enables you to easily calculate the day of the week of any day during that month. Let's assume you want to know the day of the week for August 21. Check the twelve-digit number: The first Sunday of August falls on the 4th. Simply add 7's to that number (because there are seven days in a week). If the first Sunday is the 4th, then adding a 7 tells you that the 11th is also a Sunday. Add 7 to 11, and you know that the 18th is a Sunday. Then the 19th is a Monday, the 20th is a Tuesday—and the 21st of August falls on Wednesday!

Of course, there's no need to add the 7's one by one. Add a multiple of 7; in the above example, you'd simply add 14 to 4 right away, and take it from there. The largest multiple of 7 you'll ever have to add is 28.

Suppose you want to know the day of the week on which Christmas Day falls. The first Sunday of December is the 1st; add 21, and you know that the 22nd of December is also a Sunday. So the 23rd is Monday, the 24th is Tuesday, and Christmas Day falls on a Wednesday.

Occasionally, you'll work backward. For example, find the day of the week for June 14. The first Sunday in June is the 2nd.

Add 14, and you know that the 16th is also a Sunday. That tells you that the 15th is a Saturday, and the 14th, of course, falls on a Friday.

Now try a few on your own. Find the day of the week for these dates in 1974: April 15, November 7, January 12, May 27, March 5, October 26, February 13, and September 8.

Breaking the twelve-digit number into groups of three makes it easier for you to get to a particular month quickly. After you use the idea for a short time, whenever you think of a month you'll also think of the word or phrase that includes that month. If you don't care about that, Link the number any way you like (**chum, mug, linger, dishmat** would do it).

When you get to 1975, it's easy enough to memorize the new twelve-digit number at the beginning of the year—but you don't have to. In the number for 1975, you'll see that each digit is one less than for 1974. Look:

$$1974—633\ 752\ 741\ 631$$
$$1975—522\ 641\ 637\ 527$$

Don't let those 7's (beneath the 1's) throw you. Since there is no zero day, when you subtract 1 from 1 the answer must be 7. What's really happening is this: You're subtracting a day from Sunday, which brings you to Saturday. So, for 1975, you can use the same number as 1974 and simply push your answer ahead one day. You'll be correct! If for any reason it would help you to know the day of the week for the current and the following year, you'd know both automatically—except for leap years. Another way is to use the same number and consider the digits to represent *Mondays*. Again, you'll be correct!

There is a way to keep using the same number into a leap year, like 1976, but we don't want to take the space to explain that here. You can work it out yourself if you study the numbers for other years that are listed below. You can simply memorize the new number each year. Or you can use the same number for three years (the third year, you'd push your answer forward *two* days, or consider each digit to represent *Tuesdays*), memorize the new one for a leap year, then memorize a new one, which you can use for three more years.

Here are the numbers up to 1983.

January February March	April May June	July August September	October November December
744	163	152	742—1973
633	752	741	631—1974
522	641	637	527—1975
417	426	415	375—1976 (leap year)
266	315	374	264—1977
155	274	263	153—1978
744	163	152	742—1979
632	641	637	527—1980 (leap year)
411	537	526	416—1981
377	426	415	375—1982
266	315	374	264—1983

Before leaving this idea, weekdays within years, there's another way to handle it. Make up a Substitute Word for each month, and associate that to a Peg Word that tells you the first Sunday. For January, a picture of a **jan**itor might serve as the Substitute. For the year 1974, see a gigantic **shoe** being a janitor. February? **Fib** or **fob,** and associate it to **Ma.** For March, see your **Ma march**ing. You may feel that this method is faster, or more definite. The choice is yours. Here's a suggestion or two for the remaining months:

April—ape, fool (April Fool), or showers (April showers)
May—May pole
June—bride, or chewin'
July—jewel, or firecracker (July 4)

August—gust of wind
September—scepter, or sipped
October—octopus, or oboe
November—ember, new member, or turkey (Thanksgiving)
December—Christmas tree

Whatever method you use, knowing the day of the week a future date falls on is easy, and it's fun. Test yourself now—look at the twelve-digit number for 1983 and say out loud, almost instantly, the day of the week your birthday falls on in that year.

15 ANNIVERSARIES, THE ZODIAC, HISTORICAL DATES

The same basic idea that is used for remembering a day and hour works for remembering a month and day. Any date that falls within the first ten days of the first nine months of the year breaks down to a basic Peg Word. The date May 4 would transpose to 54 (**lure**)—5th month, 4th day. March 8 transposes to **movie**, August 10 to **fuse**, January 6 to **dish**, September 3 to **bum**, and July 4 to **car**.

Any day past the 10th, and any month past September, transpose to a three-digit number. In most cases, what you'd do is make up a word to represent that three-digit number. For example, October 8 could transpose to **toss off** (10th month, 8th day); December 3 to **denim**; and so on.

But take another look at that last example. **Denim** transposes to 123, which could represent the 12th month, 3rd day. It could also, however, represent the 1st month, 23rd day.

There are, as usual, ways to solve the problem. The one we use is simply to put a zero in front of any single-digit date.

December 3, a single-digit date, is therefore represented by the digits 1203, not 123.

Now there can be no confusion; the digits 123 can represent only the 1st month (January), 23rd day. November 7 transposes to 1107, not 117, because 117 represents January 17. All you need do is think up a word or phrase for any three- or four-digit number or date.

You'll find, if you apply this idea, that the zero isn't always necessary. You could transpose May 4 to 504 (**loser, laser**), but since 54 could only represent May 4, you might just as well use **lure**. You'll have to decide whether to *always* use the zero for single-digit dates, or to use that zero only in those instances where it's needed to avoid confusion.

So. Any date can be made tangible by first breaking it down to two, three, or four digits and then coming up with a word or phrase to represent those digits phonetically. Once you understand that, all you have to do in order to remember a person's birthday or wedding anniversary is to associate the word or phrase to that person.

One way to do this is to associate the word or phrase to the person *physically*. For example, picturing your wife as a piano **tuner** would help you to remember that her birthday is January 24. (This wouldn't confuse you into thinking that the date is December 4; that would transpose to 1204, and **dancer** could represent it phonetically.)

Or you can associate the word or phrase to a Substitute Word for the person's name. To remember that Mr. Gordon's birthday is April 3, associate **ram** to **garden**. Mr. Pukczyva's birthday is March 2—see a hockey **puck shiver**ing as it shines, instead of the **moon**, in the sky.

Once you've visualized the silly picture, whenever you think of the person, you'll be reminded of the date. (We're assuming that if you care enough about someone to want to remember the birthday or anniversary, then you do think of that person every so often.)

If you think you'll have trouble remembering whether it's a birthday or anniversary date, put something into the picture to represent the correct one. A cake with candles on it would do for a birthday.

Any dates can be remembered by using this basic idea. We'll discuss historical dates in a moment, but first we'd like to show you how to apply the idea to the signs of the zodiac. So many people are interested in astrology these days that it sometimes seems everyone is asking everyone else what sign they were born under. And many people hear a birth date and then find it difficult to remember the sign for that date. But as you'll see, dates can be associated to other information—*any* information.

Here are the signs of the zodiac, the date spreads, and some suggestions for changing those dates into tangible pictures:

Aquarius	water bearer	January 20–February 18	tans, dunce–native, knot off
Pisces	fishes	February 19–March 20	net up, no lip, in a tub mince, moans
Aries	ram	March 21–April 20	mint, mount–runs, ruins
Taurus	bull	April 21–May 20	runt, rent–lens, leans
Gemini	twins	May 21–June 20	Lent, lint–shines, chins
Cancer	crab	June 21–July 20	giant, gent–cans, gains
Leo	lion	July 21–August 21	gaunt, kind–faint, found
Virgo	virgin	August 22–September 22	phone in, phonin'–banana, pinin'
Libra	scales	September 23–October 22	Pan Am, pin 'em–tossin' in, dozin' on
Scorpio	scorpion	October 23–November 22	dicin' ham, teasin' him–tide noon, tightenin'
Sagittarius	archer	November 23–December 20	deaden him–tin noise, down nose
Capricorn	goat	December 21–January 19	tenant–tote up, to type

If you want to remember all the signs, simply Link them. Either make up a Substitute Word for the sign, or, if you know the meanings, use them—they all can be pictured. For Aries, you can use **arrows, air E's,** or simply picture a ram. At this point you should be able to work this out easily for yourself.

If you don't know the meanings of the signs, associate one to the other—sign to meaning. Most of them are obvious, of course; but if you had to you could, say, associate **gem** (Gemini) to **twins.**

To remember the sign *and* date spread in each case, associate a Substitute Word for the sign, or its meaning (see Aries-ram example above), to a phrase that will give you the vital dates. For instance, a silly picture of a **ram** sucking a gigantic **mint** as it **runs** gives you both the sign and the date spread. A picture of a **corn** wearing a **cap,** or a **goat** living in your home as a **tenant** and always toting things up (**tote up**) tells you that Capricorns are born between December 21 and January 19.

As usual, you can put anything you like into your association. If you see a picture of a **bull** (Taurus or **tore ass**) being a **runt** (small bull) and very **stubbornly** breaking a gigantic **lens,** you have a reminder of the sign, the date spread, and one of the characteristics of Taurus people—stubbornness.*

Now for historical dates. Again, you already have the necessary basic knowledge. All you have to do is transpose the intangible date to a tangible picture and associate that picture to the event.

We'll start with one you already know—the date of the signing of the Declaration of Independence. A **Kaiser** (if you're using the zero in front of single digits) or a **car** (7th month, 4th day, July 4) signing the Declaration and receiving plenty of **cash** ('76) for signing it will tell you the event and the date. The assumption is that you'd know the century digits, but you can put a reminder into the association if you like. Take **cash** would do it.

*C.f. Harry Lorayne.

Usually, it isn't necessary to put the century figures into the association. You probably know that the great Chicago fire occurred in the 1800's. So a picture of a **cot** ('71) starting a great fire tells you that the date is 1871. Napoleon was crowned emperor in 1804; picture a man with his hand in his jacket (Napoleon) wearing a large crown—it's so heavy, it makes his head sore ('04). (If you like, you can picture a **dove** flying out of the crown, to remind you of 18.) The *Titanic* sank in the year 1912. Picture a large sheet of **tin** sinking; or, if you want the century figures, see it sinking in a **tub**.

Having used the states and the Presidents as examples earlier, we'll continue using them now—you can include a picture to represent any date in any of your original associations. Perhaps you want to remember the year in which a state was admitted to the Union. Nothing could be simpler. Indiana was admitted in 1816; get **dish** or **dove dish** into your original association. You **can't talk** (Kentucky) because there's a **dog bone** in your throat—this picture would remind you that Kentucky was admitted to the Union in 1792.

President Grant was born on April 27, 1822. Picture a large piece of **granite** (Substitute Word for Grant, or use **rant**) putting a **ring** (427 = April 27) on a **nun**'s ('22) finger. If you see this silly picture taking place on a **ship**, that will help you remember that President Grant was inaugurated in 1869.

William Shakespeare's baptism was recorded on April 26, 1564. See yourself shaking a **spear** in a **tall jar** (1564) on a **ranch** (April 26). If you want to remember only the month and year, **rattle jar**, or **retail chair** (4-1564) would suffice. If you already know the century, **rasher** or **reacher** would remind you of April, '64.

The first man to step onto the moon was Neil Armstrong, and he did it on July 20, 1969. A picture of a man with a **strong arm** (or just a strong muscular arm) holding hundreds of **cans** (720, July 20) would tell you the month and day. See the man (or the arm) coming out of a **ship**, and you have a reminder of the year. If you want to remember the month and year only, associate the Substitute Word for Armstrong to **ketchup** (7-'69).

If you formed an association of a **stevedore** dressed in **lace** and wrestling a **bear**, it would help you remember that Robert Louis Stevenson (stevedore) was born in 1850 (lace) and died in 1894 (bear).

Now you can remember any date by changing it to a tangible picture and associating that to the person, place, or event. Again, once you've used the memorized information a few times and it has become knowledge, the system has served its purpose—the ridiculous pictures fade because you no longer need them.

16

THE ALPHABET AND PICTURING LETTERS

HL: Arteriosclerosis!

JL: Aceeiiloorrrssst!

HL: So you've been alphabetizing words since you were eight years old—it still amazes me. What's the story, Jerry?

JL: I'm screwy. No, seriously, I basically use the Substitute Word system. When a word is alphabetized it becomes a nonsense word, so I associate a Substitute thought for the nonsense word to the regular word. "Telephone" alphabetized is "eeehlnopt," so my original picture was **eel napped** on a **telephone**. That doesn't give me all the letters, but it does give me the nonsense word. I'll know that there are three e's, and that there has to be an *h* in there somewhere.

•

Most people don't know the alphabet as well as they think they do. Few people know the numerical positions of the letters. Not that it's of great importance, but it is interesting that people use these twenty-six letters all their lives and still don't know, instantly, the numerical position of, say, **P** or **K,** or **M.**

We're going to show you how to *picture* letters. But first, here's a quick way of learning the numerical positions of all the letters. It's not just an exercise—knowing them can be important if you need an extra Peg list of words, or pictures. Once you know the numerical positions and can picture each letter, you'll automatically have a twenty-six-word Peg list.

We're assuming that you know the basic Peg Words from 1 to 26. Now, you need the "adjective" idea. Make up a phrase that consists of two words—the first word is an adjective that begins with the letter whose position you want to know; the second is the Peg Word that tells you that position.

Look at these phrases:

Awful tie
Brave Noah
Cute Ma
Delicious rye

Each phrase gives you the two things you need, the letter and its position. "Delicious rye" tells you that the letter D (first letter of *delicious*) is the fourth letter (**rye**) of the alphabet. You're better off making up your own adjectives, because the ones you think of will be easier for you to remember. Here are just a few suggestions: jagged **toes**, kind **tot**, plastic **dish**, vivacious **nun**, X-rayed **Nero**, zigzag **notch**.

When you've made up all the phrases, go over them once or twice. Here, it isn't necessary to form a ridiculous association—the *logical* aspect of the phrase will be a memory aid. Before long, if you think *P*, the phrase "**plastic dish**" will come to mind and you'll know that P is the 16th letter of the alphabet. And before much longer, you won't need the phrase—you'll simply know the numerical positions.

That's all there is to it!

Now. To visualize each letter of the alphabet—to make each letter tangible and meaningful in your mind—make up a word that sounds like the letter. This is an offshoot of the Substitute Word system. The letter A, for instance, cannot be pictured, but you can picture an **ape**. And saying the letter A out loud almost has to remind you of ape, because ape sounds like A. You can make up your own Alphabet Words, or you can use the list that follows.

1. A—ape		14. N—hen, or end
2. B—bean		15. O—eau (water), or old
3. C—sea		16. P—pea
4. D—dean		17. Q—cue (stick)
5. E—eel		18. R—hour (clock), or art
6. F—half, or effort		19. S—ess curve, or ass
7. G—jeans, or gee		20. T—tea
8. H—ache, age, or itch		21. U—ewe
9. I—eye		22. V—veal
10. J—jay (bird)		23. W—Waterloo (Napoleon)
11. K—cake, or cane		24. X—eggs, exit, or X ray
12. L—el (elevated train), elf		25. Y—wine
13. M—ham, hem, or **emperor**		26. Z—zebra

We used **bean** for B only because you already know **bee** as the basic Peg Word for number 9.

Being able to picture any letter is important if you ever have to memorize anything that contains letters—formulas and equations, style numbers, stock symbols, whatever. Now, if for some reason you wanted to remember a license number, say, 146A 29C 4L, you could Link **torch** to **ape**, ape to **knob**, knob to **sea**, sea to **rye**, and rye to **elevated train**.

If you know the numerical position of every letter *and* the alphabet word, you also have that twenty-six-word Peg List we mentioned. If you know that N is the 14th letter, anything associated to **hen** is the 14th item. Anything associated to **pea** is the 16th item, anything associated to **ess** curve is the 19th item, and so on.

Now you can memorize two lists of items—by number, and in and out of order—at the same time. Use the basic Peg Words for one list and the Alphabet Words for the other.

The fact that each letter can be pictured can be useful to you in many areas. If you're one of the many people who have trouble spelling the word *insurance* because you're never sure whether it's -*ance* or -*ence,* picture an **ape** selling insurance and you'll always remember that *insurance* is spelled with an *a*. The word *audible* is spelled with an *i* (it's not "aud*a*ble"). Form a silly picture of your **eye** making sounds—it's **audible**—to remind you of the *i*. The word *grammar* is often misspelled "grammer." Picture an **ape** speaking with perfect grammar, and you'll remember that *a*.

There are other ways to handle letters. For example, if all the style numbers of any company's products consist of a letter followed by digits, then a word that begins with the letter solves the memory problem. For A41, use **arid**; for B12, **button**; for C915, **capital**; for R92, **robin**; and so on. Each word would then be associated, of course, to the product it represents.

Finally, a nonearthshaking piece of information: If you form a Link from **zebra** to **wine** to **eggs** to **Waterloo**, all the way to **ape**, you'll be able to recite the alphabet backward!

17 *START YOUR CHILDREN*

JL: My son and daughter—Jeff's nine, Julie's eight—can remember things in sequence and by number, quickly and easily. And they're having a ball.

HL: When my son Bobby turned five this year, I tried him on ten items, with the Link. First time out, he remembered them—no hesitation, forward and backward—and he thought it was hilarious!

Not long ago, I tried the Peg on a children's TV show—the average age of the studio audience was seven—and the kids remembered ten items in and out of order, by number.

JL: Before my daughter was aware of the systems, she had trouble telling her left hand from her right. I'd ask her, "Which is your right hand, Julie?" She'd stand up and start reciting the Pledge of Allegiance, putting her right hand over her heart. Then she'd raise that hand and say, "This one, Daddy!"

•

Very young children have no trouble using their imagination and forming ridiculous pictures. They not only do it easily, they think it's lots of fun. If you have children, acquaint them with some of the ideas in this book; you can harness that lively imagination and help them sharpen their sense of concentration—without their realizing what you're doing, of course.

Make a game out of the Link system. During an automobile

trip, see who can remember a list of items faster, or who can remember the most items. It *is* fun—and the children are learning a useful skill at the same time.

If you want to play the game of remembering items by number with a child who's too young to learn the phonetic alphabet, there's a way to teach him ten Peg Words almost instantly. They're easy to learn—they rhyme with the numbers, and most of them come from a song your children probably know.

1. one—run
2. two—shoe
3. three—tree
4. four—pour
5. five—hive (picture bees)
6. six—sticks
7. seven—heaven
8. eight—gate
9. nine—sign
10. ten—hen

Some of the words from the song have been changed to words that are easier for a child to picture. Teach the youngster to picture the item running, for 1 (**run**); being poured out of something, for 4 (**pour**); in the sky, for 7 (**heaven**); and so on.

The number-word rhymes make it easy for a child to learn the words in minutes. Once he has been tested on them, and knows them, he can be taught to associate (don't use that word; the children won't know what you're talking about) any item to any of these Pegs. If you mention **banana** for number 6, the child will think **sticks** and, perhaps, see a bunch of bananas tied like a bunch of sticks. Give him a suggestion or two the first few times.

Here's another way to use the Link as a game. Place eight or so items on a tray and cover them with a cloth. First remove the cloth for a short time (a minute or so), then replace it and have everyone try to list all the items. Each player receives one point for each item listed correctly; the more a player lists, the better his score.

Or you can show the items for a moment, then remove a couple of them without letting the players see which ones have been removed. You expose the tray of items again for ten seconds or so. The first player who correctly lists the missing items wins. Both these games are fun for children and teach them to start using some important mental powers—observation, memory, and concentration. They also work as incentives for the child to try to apply a simple Link.

You can also start helping the child to remember words through the Substitute Word system. When five-year-old Bobby Lorayne kept saying "caterlipper" for caterpillar, he was told to picture a **cat** chasing the crawling thing up a **pillar** (or **pillow**). It worked!

Surely every parent has used something of this sort at one time or another. But now you can take it much further. Use Substitute Words, with the child, for English or foreign words. It's amazing how well the system works with children.

Here's another game that children enjoy. In this one, pairs of letters are called or written, and each pair is assigned a hiding place. For example, PN is called, and the hiding place is the fish tank; FX is hidden in the TV set; CP in the window; TR in the flower pot, and so on. The child who remembers the most pairs of letters wins.

Tell the child to think of a word that begins and ends with the vital letters and then associate, in a silly way, that word (or thing) to the hiding place. The child might picture a gigantic **pin** swimming in the fish tank, a **fox** jumping out of the TV screen, a gigantic **cup** crashing through a window, and **tar** overflowing from, and ruining, a flower pot.

Any word can be used that will remind the child of the letters. If the letters are BN, **bin** is fine—but **bone** would still help the child remember them. For TR, **tire** or **tree** would also do.

The game encourages the child to think of letters and words and get them right, helps his memory, and is fun to play. Children love to win; they'll learn just because they want to play and win.

You can take this particular game a step further by using two letters plus a number from 1 to 10. Use the ten rhyming Pegs for this. If you call PT and number 5, hidden in the kitchen sink, the child might see a ridiculous picture of himself turning the faucet in the kitchen sink, and millions of **pits** and bees (hive-five) coming out of it.

There's an old game in which each player adds an item to a list. The first player might say, "I'm going to Indianapolis to get a bottle." The next player says, "I'm going to Indianapolis to get a bottle and a desk." The third player says, "I'm going to Indianapolis to get a bottle, a desk, and a fish." The game can be played with any number of players, each of whom must repeat all the items correctly and add one item. If there are four players, the first person's turn comes up again after the fourth person. The first player who misses an item is "out"; the last person "in" wins. The application of the Link to this old game gives it a new dimension. With a little thought, any game can be changed or made more challenging by using such memory systems as the Link, Substitute Words, and Peg Words.

Starting young children off on some of the principles of a trained memory is one of the most useful things you can do for them. Imagine how helpful the systems can be to them for play, in school (most schoolwork is based on memory), and, later, socially and professionally.

18 *SPORTS*

JL: Not just any professional basketball player, regardless of his abilities, could play for the New York Knickerbockers. The Knicks win championships because we're a team in the true sense of the word—the five players on the floor at any given time play for the good of all and not for themselves. That's really the only way to keep winning in pro basketball.

HL: You're a smart team, too—intelligence must be a factor.

JL: Sure it is. The basic intelligence of our players, and their basketball savvy, are actually more important than most people realize. We're not an overpowering type of team, so we have to depend on other assets—like playing unselfishly, playing intelligently, and generally outthinking our opponents. In order for us to win consistently, the five men on the floor have to think and act almost as one person. This means that each player must know what his teammates are going to do in almost every situation. A good part of this is knowing the plays we'll be running—if a play is called and one or two of the players don't remember it, the results can be disastrous.

HL: How often do the plays get called?

JL: We attempt to run a basic play every time we come down the floor, unless we have an obvious breakaway situation that will lead to an easy basket. This strategy gives us much more consistency—and leaves us in better defensive balance if we miss the shot and the other team rebounds the ball.

HL: You're really saying that none of you can perform well unless you remember the plays well. I know how *you* remember them—but what about your teammates?

JL: Fundamentally, the other players use rote memory. We all go over and over the plays throughout the year, to make sure everybody knows them. And for the Knicks, that's maybe a total of forty plays and options.

HL: How well does the method work?

JL: This may seem hard to believe, but I've never played on a basketball team at any level including the professional level without at least one player forgetting several of the plays all the way through the season. Many times, there are several players who don't remember them.

At some crucial point in a game, the coach will tell the players during a time-out what play he wants to run, why it's important that each player know exactly what his assignment is and carry it out. So. We break, we don't take three or four steps out on the floor, and a player taps me on the shoulder—he knows I remember all the plays—and says, "What are we doing? What play are we calling?" And that has happened, and does happen, over and over again.

HL: Obviously, those players aren't very aware. And just as obviously, since they turn to you when they forget, the systems work for you in basketball.

JL: I use them to remember all our plays. And any player *could* use them to remember what he's supposed to do during any particular play.

•

For obvious reasons, we'll begin our discussion of memory in sports with basketball. First, a play we'll designate play number

6. Most plays in basketball are called out by number, and it's a simple matter to associate that play to the basic Peg Word.

The diagram on the following page shows what play number 6 might look like after a coach has explained it:

If you ignore all the arrows, dashes, and lines in the diagram, you'll see the basic positioning of a team. C is center; LF and LG are left forward and left guard; RF and RG are right forward and right guard.

Now. A dotted line (‑‑‑‑‑‑‑‑‑►) is a pass made with the ball; a solid line (————————►) is the direction in which the player moves; the solid short lines (\ ) are picks or blocks by one of the players.

RG starts with the ball. He passes it to LG who, in turn, passes it to LF. LF then passes the ball to C. If you follow the dotted lines and arrows, you can follow the ball's progress as it is being passed.

As soon as LF passes the ball to C, he starts to move toward the middle of the court. At the same time, LG starts to move toward the *end* of the court. Both LF and LG are also moving toward C. Now, LF momentarily stops to pick or block LG's opponent and then continues to the middle of the court where he picks RF's opponent as RF moves toward the middle of the court to join LF.

LF then turns and moves toward the basket after he picks for RF. While all this is going on, LG (if he hasn't gotten the ball from C, for a shot) circles under the basket and back toward the middle of the floor. RG moves away from the action in order to keep his opponent from interfering with the play.

C has several options during this play. The first is to pass the ball to LG when LF picks for him. The second option is to pass to RF when LF picks for him. The third is to pass the ball to LF as he moves to the basket after he has picked for RF. Finally, if none of these options is available, C can turn and shoot the ball himself.

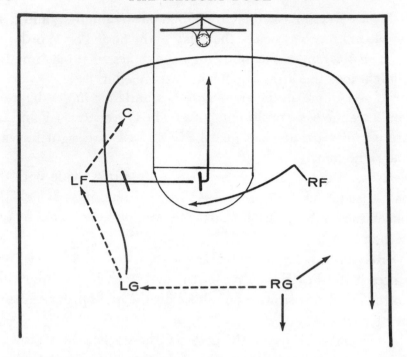

In this one basic play, you can see that there are several options for (hopefully) good open shots during its execution. Each player has specific duties to remember:

C —Get to basic position.
   Receive ball from LF.
   Pass ball to LG, RF, or LF.
   If play doesn't work, shoot.

LF—Receive ball from LG.
   Pass ball to C.
   Move toward C and pick for LG.
   Move toward middle and pick for RF.
   Move to basket.

LG—Receive pass from RG.
   Pass to LF.
   Move off LF's pick, to the basket.
   If no shot develops, circle back under basket to original position.

RF—Move off the pick by LF to center of floor.
Look for pass from C and shoot if open.
RG—Pass to LG.
Move away from play.

It would be a simple task for each player to Link, or associate, his duties to **shoe** (6). All he need do is make up a few standards to represent the positions. Any words containing the proper letters would do. C could be **c**ore (picture an apple core. It begins with *c,* and also means center); LF could be **l**ea**f**; RF could be **r**oo**f**; LG could be **l**o**g**; RG could be **r**u**g**.

The best way to memorize the play described above is to use one picture; no Link is necessary for so short a play. C could picture a **shoe** moving to a **basic** position. (He could simply see it moving to *his* basic position, or he could put **base**, **sick**, or both, into the picture.) A **leaf** throws a ball to the shoe and the shoe looks around at a **log**, a steeple (**roof**), and a gigantic **leaf**, trying to decide which one to throw it to. It can't decide, so it **shoots** itself!

Check back to C's duties for this play, and you'll see that this silly picture will quickly remind the center of them. When he's on the floor and a player or coach calls "Six," he'll instantly know what he has to do. (Bear in mind that this is all the players need—reminders.)

LF might picture a **shoe** receiving a ball from a **log**; the shoe throws the ball at an apple **core** as he moves toward that core, and **picks** up a **log** and a **roof**; he places a shoe into a **basket**. (We consider this to be one picture. A Link would work as well: shoe to log to core to pick to log to roof to shoe to basket.)

LG: a **shoe** catches a ball thrown by a **rug** and immediately throws it to a **leaf**; it **picks** up the leaf as it moves toward a **basket** in **circles**.

RF: a **shoe** moves off a **pick** held by a **leaf**; it moves to the **middle** of the floor; an apple **core** makes a **pass** at the shoe; the shoe **shoots**

RG: a **shoe** throws a ball to a **log**, then moves out of sight.

The player would form associations or Links like these in order to originally remember all the team plays. After a few uses, the pictures will fade as usual; he'll simply *know* the plays.

In football, the plays are more complicated because there are eleven men on a team. But a play still involves each man's remembering what he himself is supposed to do during any called play. The exception would be the quarterback, who should pretty much be aware of what each of his teammates is supposed to do, and where they're supposed to be. To help him originally memorize the play, his Links would be a bit more involved.

The same kind of associations or Links will help any player to be Originally Aware of his duties. This is what a diagram of play number 14, the "dive-option" play, might look like on a coach's blackboard:

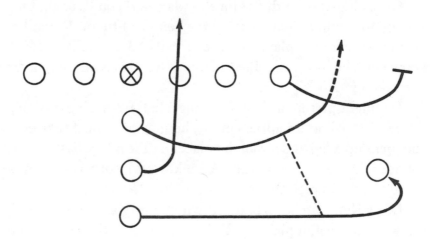

Here are the basic duties of the three key men in this particular play:

QB (quarterback)—Open pivot, ride the FB, read first man outside tackle for handoff, option the end man on the line of scrimmage.

FB (fullback)—Dive over the guard, mesh with the QB. If ball is received, run to daylight; if not, fake through line and block.

TB (tailback)—Take counter step and run option course maintaining 7-yard relationship with QB.

Originally, each player might have formed a Link, starting either with a **dive**—if the quarterback simply called for "dive option" in the huddle—or with **tire**, if the play was called by number. A player might simply need to know that play 14 is the dive-option play. In that case, he would originally have associated tire to dive.

QB's Link could be: A tire (or dive) is **open**ing a ballet dancer's (Substitute thought for **pivot**) costume; an empty costume is riding on a gigantic watch fob (**FB**); a gigantic fob is reading a **hand** (handoff) that's throwing fishing **tackle outside**; the hand is trying to decide (**option**) who is the last (**end**) man in a **line** (of scrimmage).

The FB's Link: A tire dives over a **guard**rail, into a mess (**mesh**) of **quarters** (QB); it grabs a quarter and runs toward a **light**—it drops the quarter (doesn't receive the ball) onto a **fake line** of **blocks**.

The TB's Link: A tire **steps** on a **counter** (or someone steps on a counter in order to dive) and runs **up** a **chin** (option) to meet his **relation**, a gigantic **cow** (7-yard **relation**ship); the cow is giving **quarters** instead of milk.

In baseball, a batter must remember that the signal for, say, hit and run, is the coach rubbing his elbow. He'd simply picture an elbow hitting someone and running away. Each day, the player has to remember that day's "key" signal, the signal that means, "If I do this, then the next sign is really to be followed."

If the coach doesn't use the "key," the player ignores any other signal. So. The player could simply associate a **key** to whatever the key signal is for that day. There might also be a "wipeout" signal, a sign that means, "Ignore the signal I just gave you." Same thing; the player would associate **wipe** or **wipeout** to the signal.

One announcer at a trotters track used the systems for years to help him call the races. He needed to know horses' names, jockeys' names, horses' numbers, and colors for every race. He associated all the information to each horse's number, starting a Link with the number. He used a standard for every color—a **bull** might represent red, an **orange** could represent orange, a **banana** could represent yellow, **grass** could represent green, a **grape** could represent purple, and so on. In this way, even colors can be pictured.

We've been using examples from the participant's point of view. But if you're a sports fan, you can apply the same ideas to whatever information or statistics you want to remember. Babe Ruth's career home-run record is 714. Picture a gigantic **baby** playing a **guitar** at **home**; or, the home is in the **gutter**. See a **green** ice**berg** that's **maimed**, and that picture will help you remember that Hank Greenberg hit 331 homers in his career.

Who was the world's heavyweight boxing champ in 1936? You'll remember James Braddock if you associate **match** (36) to, perhaps, **haddock** or **bad dock**. Associate **mummy** to **carnival** or **car near** to remind you that Primo Carnera was the heavyweight champ in 1933. Picture a **bear** using a lawn **mower** to tell you that Max Baer was the 1934 champ.

In what year was the famous Dempsey-Firpo fight? Associate **damp sea** and **fir pole** to **name**—1923. If you want to remember the exact date, use **butter name**: 9-14-23.

As you can see, the memory systems can be applied just as easily to sports as to anything else.

19 THE STOCK MARKET

HL: Much of the information people in the market need to know, such as stock symbols, is purely and simply a memory problem. A student of mine once wanted to leave his menial job and obtain a position with a brokerage house. He used the Substitute Word and Alphabet Word system to memorize the symbol of every stock traded on the New York Stock Exchange—about 1,600 at the time.

He applied for the job, and found he had plenty of competition. During the interview, he handed the stock exchange listings to his potential employer and asked him to call off any company or symbol. Whichever was called, he named its counterpart instantly—without missing a one.

JL: I assume he got the job.

HL: The interviewer told him, "There are people who've been working here for years, and not one of them knows all the symbols—you're hired!" Today, that former student of mine is co-owner of his own company in the put-and-call area.

JL: I'll remember that when I'm over the hill for basketball!

•

People involved in the stock market (clients and brokers) must be able to remember a great deal of information, including names of companies, their stock symbols, and, of course, prices. You should know how to handle prices now. Make up a word or phrase for the price, then associate it to the name of the stock. That's easy enough. The only additional problem involved is that of handling the fractions.

This problem is easily solved if you change all fractions to eighths, which is the common denominator of stock market price fractions. You'd be dealing, then, with: 1/8, 2/8 (¼), 3/8, 4/8 (½), 5/8, 6/8 (¾), and 7/8.

The pattern you follow, basically, is to make up a word that tells you the dollars—a word whose last single consonant sound tells you the number of eighths (the fraction). For a stock selling at 29½, picture the word **napper** or **nipper** and you've got that price. The first two consonant sounds can only represent 29, the final consonant sound **r** (4) reminds you of the number of eighths—4, in this example, and you know that 4/8 is ½.

You may be wondering how you would know that **nipper** represents 29½, not 294. Well, if you aren't knowledgeable enough to know that a stock that's been fluctuating around $29 can't be selling at $294 you shouldn't be in the stock market! So, your knowledge of the market plus your common sense tells you the difference. If you had associated, say, **racket** to a gigantic telephone (AT&T), you'd know that **racket** represents 47 1/8, not 471.

As usual, there are other methods you can use. If you like, you can always use a phrase to represent a price; the first word for the dollars, followed by a Peg Word to tell you the number of eighths. That way, 29½ could transpose to **knob rye** or **nip rye**, and 47⅛ to **rack tie** or **rock tie**. This method leaves you with no decisions to make.

Of course, you may not care about the fractions at all; you may only need to know the price in dollars. Just forget about the fractions and use a word to represent only dollars.

Whichever method you decide to use will work. Associate the word to the company name by using a Substitute Word or thought to represent the company—**telephone** would certainly remind you of AT&T. A **car** saluting a **general** might be your Substitute thought for General Motors. A tiny bottle of soda (**mini soda**) wearing a **miners'** hat could remind you of Minnesota Mining; **spare a hand** would do for Sperry Rand; **polar hurt** for Polaroid; **Mack roar E** for McCrory Corporation; and so on.

So. An association of a **Mack** truck **roaring** at an **E** (or **eel**) that's sitting on a **melon** would remind you that McCrory stock was selling at 35¼.

What about remembering stock symbols? The stockbroker has a machine on his desk that will give him current prices pretty quickly—*if* he punches the *correct* symbol. A broker who could instantly recall any stock symbol he needed to know would have an advantage.

Now, you probably don't want or need to remember all the symbols. But if you want to remember some of them, it's easy.

Just make up a word or phrase to represent the letters of the symbol. There are two ways to do this—you can use a word that reminds you of the letters, or you can use the Alphabet Words. For example, the symbol for Pittway Corporation is PRY. You might see a gigantic **pit prying** its **way** out of something—the association gives you the two pieces of information you need, the name of the company and its symbol. Associating Pittway to a **pea** on a clock (**hour**) drinking **wine** would accomplish the same thing.

Picture a **polly** (parrot) being a **Ma** to a **plum**, and you have a reminder that the symbol for Polymer Corporation is PLM.

The symbol for Shaw Industries is SHX; you might picture millions of **eggs** (X) coming up on a **shore**—you say "**Sh**" to them. Whatever reminder you think of will work; you could have used "**shucks**" to remind you of SHX. An **ass** (S) scratching an **itch** (H) with an **exit** (X) sign would also do.

Picture a **hen** and an **eel** eating a **ham** on a **new mountain** to help you remember that the symbol for Newmont Mining is

NEM. If you really think it's necessary, include something in the picture to remind you of mining.

You can form an association that includes the name of the company, the symbol, the average price of the stock (or the price you paid), the name of the top executive of the company—whatever you like.

The point is that now you can *picture* letters. Picturing either the Alphabet Words, or a word that begins and ends with or contains the vital letters, is tantamount to picturing the letters.

The same ideas can be used wherever you find it necessary to remember letters in conjunction with anything else.

20 *POLITICS*

JL: It's too bad we can't drop the names of some politicians who use our systems.

HL: They wouldn't allow it—and you can't blame them. They'd never be able to get by with sitting in front of a congressional or Senate committee and saying, "I don't remember"!

•

It's obvious that being able to remember names and faces is an asset to any politician, just as it is to businessmen. But a politician should be able to remember a great many other things— certainly he should have all the political information, at least for his home state, at his fingertips. Most of this information is statistical and involves names and numbers. The systems, of course, apply to both areas.

Most people do not know the names of their representatives and senators. If you're among them, simply make up a Substitute Word to represent senator—**tore** (picture tearing), **centaur**, or **century** would do.

The senators from Nevada (elected in 1970) are Bible and Cannon. See yourself **tearing** a gigantic **bible** and getting shot by a **cannon** for your crime. That does it. If you're not from Nevada, but still want to know who its senators are, get a Substitute Word for the state into the picture. You can take it further. If you want to remember party affiliations, make up a standard to represent each major party. Obviously, you can use an elephant (R) or a donkey (D), since those are the party symbols. Or, use **dean** (D) and **hour** (R), the Alphabet Words, or **dam** for Democrat and **pub** for Republican. In this example, if you're using the Alphabet Words for your standard, you'd get whatever you picture for dean into the association with Bible and Cannon, both of whom are Democrats.

Many people have trouble remembering which symbol belongs to which party. They're reminded of the donkey and elephant symbols during national conventions, but a short time after the election they're no longer sure. (It's rather like trying to remember last year's Academy Award winners.) One fast association of, say, elephant to **pub**—and you'll always know that the elephant is the symbol of the Republican party and, of course, the donkey is the Democratic symbol.

The senators from Ohio (all these examples are as of 1970 records) are Taft and Saxbe. You might see a **daft** (Taft) **centaur** playing a **sax**ophone. That's probably all you need to remind you of Saxbe, but if you like, you can see a **bee** coming out of the saxophone. They're both Republicans, so you can get elephant, hour, or pub into the picture for each name.

Suppose you want to remember how many representatives your state has. Using Ohio again as the example, it has 24 representatives—7 Democrats and 17 Republicans. One easy way to apply the system to such information is to always use a word that ends with a *d* or an *r* for Democrat and Republican—a word whose first consonant sound or sounds tell you how many Democrats and Republicans there are.

Good, goad, or **cod** would mean 7 Democratic representatives; **tiger, dagger,** or **ticker** would tell you that there are 17 Republican representatives. Of course, if all you want to know is the total number of representatives, just use a word that begins or ends with *r*. Once you decide where you'll place the vital letter, always use it that way and the word will work for you.

The word **runner** would work for Ohio if you're placing the *r* first. The next consonant sound or sounds gives you the number of representatives.

You'd be surprised to see how easily you can remember the number of representatives from each state this way. Once you've made up the word that tells you the number, just associate that to your Substitute Word for the state. Try a few:

New York has 41 representatives. Associate **new cork** or the Empire State Building to **roared** or **reared.**

Oklahoma has 6 representatives. Associate **homer** to **rash** or **roach.**

Alabama has 8 representatives. Associate **album** to **roof** or **rave.**

Nebraska has 3 representatives. Associate **new brass car** to **room** or **ram.**

Texas has 43 representatives. Associate **taxis** to **rearm** or **roar 'em.**

Pennsylvania has 27 representatives. Associate **pencil** to **rink** or **ring.**

Tennessee has 9 representatives. Associate **tennis** to **rope** or **ripe.**

Kentucky has 7 representatives. Associate **can't talk** to **rag** or **rug.**

Massachusetts has 12 representatives. See a **mass chewing** something that's **rotten.**

Including Ohio (**high** or "**oh, hi**" to **runner**), you have ten examples. Form the associations, then test yourself—you'll probably know the number of representatives from each of those ten states.

If you're involved (or just interested) in national politics, you might find it useful to know the number of registered Democratic voters in particular states. No problem; just as you could remember the population of, say, Tennessee by associating **tennis** to **ma banner touch 'er,** or **moppin' red chair** (3,924,164), you can associate a state to the number that represents the Democratic (or Republican, or both) registered voters. If you formed an association of a **new brass car** delivering a **message** to a **new nail**, it would help you remember that there are 306,225 registered Democrats in Nebraska. Get **my love jailer** into the picture, along with either **pub, elephant,** or **hour,** and you'll know that there are 358,654 registered Republicans. If all you need to remember is the total registration, make up a phrase to represent 664,879 and associate it to Nebraska.

At this point you should have no difficulty in working out a method to help you remember the number of state senators and/or assemblymen in your state. New York State's state senate consists of 57 senators—25 Democrats and 32 Republicans. Associate **denial** (D, 25) and **Roman** (R, 32) to your Substitute Word for state senate. If you're doing this with more than one state, get your Substitute Word or phrase for New York into the picture. Associate **decked, ducat, ducked** (D, 71) and **rake up, recoup,** or **rag pie** (R, 79) to a Substitute Word for assembly, and you'll know the affiliation breakdown of assemblymen. For California: state senate, 21 Democrats (**donut**) and 19 Republicans (**retap,** or **retape**); state assembly, 43 Democrats (**dream** or **drum**) and 37 Republicans (**remake** or **room key**).

In a quick check we asked twenty-five people, from eighteen different states, if they knew how many electoral votes their home states controlled in a presidential election. Not one person knew! And a few of them were involved in politics. All that's necessary is to associate a state to a one- or two-digit number.

If you're remembering other information as well, get a word into your association or Link that tells you the two things you want to know: 1) that it's electoral votes you're remembering, 2) how many votes. Either start the word with an *e* for electoral or end it with an *e,* or an *-el.* Oklahoma has 8 electoral votes; **elf** or **fuel,** according to the pattern you intend to use, would give you that information.

Let's assume you decide to *start* each word with an *e*. For some two-digit numbers, there may not be a word to fit. For example, Pennsylvania has 27 electoral votes. Finding a word that starts with *e* and whose consonant sounds only represent 27 may be difficult if not impossible. Simply use a word like **enc**lose—as was the case when we discussed letter-exchange telephone numbers. Since you know that no state has electoral votes comprising three digits (the largest is California, with 45), you'd simply ignore the sounds that follow **enc**.

If you're familiar with our systems, you'll see when you sit down with any memory problem that you can easily patternize the problem so that one or another of the systems applies.

Associate **mix again** to **end** and you'll know that Michigan has 21 electoral votes. **Sassy can** to **egg** (Kansas, 7); **high** to **enlarge** (Ohio, 25); **whiz con** to **edit** (Wisconsin, 11); **wash** to **ebb** (Washington, 9); **potato** to **car** (Idaho, 4); **caliph** to **early** (California, 45); and so on.

All the suggestions in this chapter have been just that— suggestions. The way you patternize any memory problem is up to you. And, usually, the method you select to handle any memory problem will be the best for you.

21 *THE ARTS*

By now, you should realize that the systems are applicable to just about any kind of memory problem. And, as you've learned, most memory problems basically break down to entities of two. If you'd like to gain some knowledge of art, literature, or music, you might want to learn and associate artist and period, title of painting and artist, literary work and author, or piece of music and composer.

If you wanted to remember that Marcel Duchamp was of the dadaist school of painting, you would associate a Substitute Word or phrase for Duchamp to a Substitute thought for dada. Seeing a **toe chomp**ing on a baby crying for its **da da** might do it for you. Or, you could use **two champs** or **due champs** to remind you of Duchamp.

Braque and Picasso were cubists. See yourself **breaking** with a **rock** (Braque) a gigantic **cube** with a **pickax** (Picasso).

Monet and Renoir were impressionists. You might picture old **money** (Monet) being **renewed** (Renoir) to appear as an **impressionist** (one who does impersonations or impressions).

Of course, for each of the last two examples, you could associate one artist at a time to the school or period. You'd simply associate first Braque and then Picasso to cubism.

Rembrandt was a humanist. You might picture a **ram branding** a **human**.

Van Gogh and Cézanne were postimpressionists. One picture of a **van** going to **press** a **post** and **seize Ann** would do it. Or, use two separate associations; a van goes to press a post, and a **post** that's **pressing** clothes (ironing) **sees Ann**.

Edvard Munch (pronounced *Muhnk)* was an expressionist. Picture this: You're trying to **express** yourself to a **monk**.

Dali is a surrealist. Picture a **doll** that's "**sure real**." Dali is often considered to be a superrealist, so you can see that **doll** being **real** and eating **soup**.

An example of a nonobjective painter is Kandinsky. You might form a silly association of **candy** skiing and throwing **object**s at a **nun**; or **can did ski** to nonobjective.

Jackson Pollock's work is considered abstract-expressionist, or action painting. Picture a gigantic **pole lock**ed in a room where it **obstructs** (abstract) all **expression** and **action**. Or, a **pole** with a **lock** on it is being very **active** (running) and **obstruct**ing **express** trains.

Rauschenberg is a pop artist; picture a **roach** on an ice**berg** drinking soda **pop**.

Rousseau was of the primitive school of painting. Associate a **trousseau** or **Ruth sew** to **primitive** (see Ruth sewing primitive clothes). One of Rousseau's well-known paintings is "The Dream." Get something into your picture to represent dream, and you'll be reminded of that, too.

Mondrian was a constructivist; perhaps you'd like to remember that one of his paintings is titled "Broadway Boogie-Woogie." Picture a **man dryin'** a huge **construction** as he dances the **boogie-woogie** on **Broadway**.

Picturing a lot of **blue poles** (color blue, or sad blue) that are **lock**ed up will remind you that Pollock painted "Blue Poles."

See a gigantic **doll** sitting on a flying horse (**Pegasus**) to remind you that Dali did "Pegasus in Flight." If you didn't know the name of the mythical winged horse, you could use a **pea in gay sauce** for Pegasus.

Botticelli painted the "Birth of Venus." Perhaps you'd picture the **bot**tom of a **cello** (Botticelli) giving **birth** to a lady without arms (**Venus**). Select your own Substitute Words, of course. **Bottle sell E, bought a cello**, or **bought jelly** would also remind you of Botticelli, and **wean us** or the planet would remind you of Venus. Botticelli also painted "Calumny." Associate your Substitute thought for Botticelli to **column knee**.

In music appreciation, the approach is basically the same. Now that you have the idea, you won't need so many examples of ways to associate composer and composition.

Schönberg's "Violin Concerto": A **con** who's stolen a **violin** bangs it against a **chair** on a **shiny** ice**berg**.

Wagner's *Tannhäuser:* Someone crashes a **wagon** into a **townhouse**. Wagner also composed *Lohengrin.* Associate your Substitute thought for Wagner to **low and grin** or **lone grin**.

Associate **straw win ski** to **pet rush car** and a **bird** on **fire** to help you remember that Stravinsky composed "Petrouchka" and "Firebird." Get **write off spring** into the picture, and you'll also remember that he composed "Rite of Spring." You can, of course, form a Link starting with the composer and including as many of his works as you want to remember. The same method, of course, works for paintings.

Picture a **rose** growing out of your **knee** and putting a **large O** on a **totem** pole, and you'll remember that Rossini wrote "Largo al Factotum." Picture that rose getting its hair cut by a **barber** who is **civil** (or just **barber**) to remind you that Rossini wrote *The Barber of Seville.*

Liszt wrote "La Campanella"; see a **list camping on Ella**. Picture that list being very **grand** and **march**ing with a **crow** on a **mat** to remember that he also wrote "Grande Marche Chromatique."

Grieg's *Peer Gynt:* see yourself **peer**ing (with a **squint,** if you like) into a **creek.**

Brahms's "Hungarian Dances": Picture **brahma** bulls (or **bare arms**) doing **Hungarian dances,** or **danc**ing even though they're **hungry.** The "Hungarian Dances" were written as piano duets; you can see the dancing being done on two pianos. Associate the bulls or bare arms to **lead, best leader,** or just **best leader** to remind you that Brahms wrote the "Liebeslieder" waltzes.

Debussy's "La Mer": You might see a **D** being **busy** (or **bossy**) to a **llama.**

You can associate a book title to its author just as you associated artists to periods and paintings, or compositions to their composers.

The Invisible Man was written by Ralph Ellison. The author's last name is usually all you need, but you can put both names into your picture if you want to. You might picture a large, **rough** (Ralph) letter L being your son (**L is son**), and fading (becoming **invisible**).

For *The Magic Barrel,* written by Bernard Malamud: See yourself **mailing mud** in a **barrel** that's performing **magic** tricks. For a reminder of the first name, get **burn hard** into your picture.

For *Dangling Man* (Saul Bellow): See yourself **bellow**ing at a **dangling man.** Or, see yourself **below** a dangling man.

For *Rabbit Run* (John Updike): Picture a **rabbit run**ning **up a dike.**

For *Catcher in the Rye* (J. D. Salinger): A baseball **catcher** is **sailin'** a **jaw** in **rye** whiskey.

For *The Power and the Glory* (Graham Greene): Picture a

graham cracker turning **green** as it uses all its **power** to lift an American flag (Old **Glory**).

One of Robert Lowell's best-known poems is "Skunk Hour"; if you see a letter **L** sinking **low** and sniffing a clock (**hour**) that smells like a **skunk**, you shouldn't have any trouble remembering it.

To remind you that T. S. Eliot wrote "The Waste Land," you might see a gigantic cup of **tea** (T) driving an **ess** curve (S) around a huge **lot** that's a **waste land**.

Picture a **burro** eating a **naked** person for **lunch**, and you'll know that William Burroughs wrote *The Naked Lunch*.

See a gigantic fly with **gold ink** all over it being the **lord** of the other **flies**, and you won't forget that William Golding wrote *Lord of the Flies*.

And so on. The only reason we've included so many examples is for your use, if you like, as a drill or test. You can, as usual, include any information in an association: dates, names of characters, plot, theme, whatever. It doesn't matter how difficult the material seems to be; so long as you can come up with Substitute Words or phrases, you'll find it easier to remember. Where a lot of information is involved, form a Link. For example:

One of Euripides' plays is *Alcestis*. First, associate **you rip D's** to **Al says this**. The setting of the play is outside the palace at Pherae. Start a Link—associate Al says this to a **fairy** outside a **palace**. The characters are Apollo, Death, the chorus (the old men of Pherae), Alcestis, Admetus, Eumelus, Heracles, Pheres, a manservant. You might continue your Link this way: **fairy** to **apple low** to **dies** (Death) to **chorus of old men** to **Al says this** to **add my toes** to **you mail us** to **hairy keys** to **ferries** to **servant**.

How you use the systems—and what you apply them to—has

to be up to you, of course. If you're interested in the arts and want to remember all sorts of information, the systems will be invaluable time-savers. If you're not that art-minded but you would like to remember certain names, titles, and periods—why not? Memorize whatever facts you like, and you'll be able to "talk" art knowledgeably.

22   *MUSIC FOR BEGINNERS*

HL: I was about to say music is Greek to me, but that's not true. I know some Greek, and I know absolutely nothing about music—I can't sing "Happy Birthday" on key. I've found it difficult to get musical memory examples for students. I ask professional musicians, and it's hard for them to bring their minds back to the beginning, when memory was important.

JL: I know what you mean, because I don't know the first thing about music either. And I'm sure it would be hard for a professional basketball player to set down the fundamentals of the game for a beginner.

HL: Right. A professional performs by instinct. If he had to stop to remember, he'd be in trouble. But at the beginning, when he's first learning the fundamentals, memory must come into play.

•

This chapter is dedicated to all those children—and adults—who never learned the fundamentals of music because learning them involved so much drudgery and boredom. Music teachers and professional musicians tell us that most beginners who give up music do so because of the memory chores—they drop out before music becomes fun. Whether you teach these memory ideas to a child or use them yourself, you'll see that they make the study of music easier *and more fun* at the beginning. Although we'll be touching on only a few fundamentals, you'll also see that the ideas can be applied to them all.

To play a basic, three-note chord, you have to remember two notes along with the note you want to play. There are only seven *basic* notes to remember. This may not seem like much of a problem, but it is something you must know (remember) at the beginning. Every fundamental is basically a memory problem, hence the cliché among some music teachers: At the beginning, you learn "rote to note." So, although the memory problem may never be discussed, it's there all the same.

Let's start with piano. We assume here that you're familiar with the pattern of black and white keys on the piano keyboard; that you know the keyboard is divided into octaves, each beginning and ending with C, and so on.

First, you need to know the seven basic (white) notes on the keyboard—easy to remember because they're alphabetized: CDEFGAB. But remembering where, say, F is on the keyboard is a memory problem at the beginning. It must be, or memory aids like the following one wouldn't have been devised:

> All the G and A keys
> Are between the black threes
> And 'tween the twos are all the D's;
> Then on the right side of the threes
> Will be found the B's and C's;
> But on the left side of the threes
> Are all the F's and all the E's.

A better way would be to assign numbers to keys. Middle C is at the center of the keyboard. In this diagram, we've numbered the black keys as well but will, for the moment, use only whole (white) notes as examples.

All you have to do now is to associate a note (letter) to a number, and you'll remember which key to hit for that note. Picture **half** (Alphabet Word for F) a **shoe**, and you'll know that

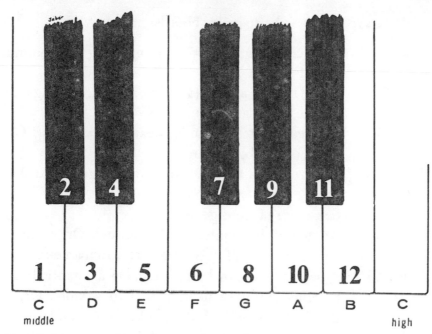

F is the key numbered 6 on the keyboard. Or, make up a word that starts with the note and ends with the number; fish for F, dam for D, and so on. Chords can be remembered the same way; picture the **sea** (Alphabet Word) with a gigantic tealeaf on it, and you'll know that playing keys 1, 5, and 8 gives you a C chord.

Try this method with the other white notes, and you'll soon *know* them—the numbers and associations will fade from your mind.

Once you do know the position of the notes, there's an easy way to memorize chords. To play a C chord, you'd have to remember to play C, E, and G. We're going to list the most common major chords, along with suggestions to help you remember each of them. In the list, you'll notice the symbol ♯ for sharp; F♯ is F-sharp. (Sharping a note makes it higher, but not as high as the next highest note—F♯ is higher than F, but not quite a G.) Now. To remember these chords easily, you form a ridiculous association for each—but you'll also need to add a standard to remind you of sharp. A **knife**, or **cutting**, will do.

Here are the seven basic major chords:

C—C E G   Associate ocean (sea = C) to **egg** (egg will remind you of EG).

D—D F♯ A   Dean, half (F) a knife (♯), ape. (A dean, holding half a knife, fights an ape.)

E—E G♯ B   Eel, jeans cut by a knife, bean. Or, an **egg** (EG) being cut (♯) by a bean.

F—F A C   Picture half a **face**. Or, half an ape goes into the sea.

G—G B D   See a pair of jeans going **bad**.

A—A C♯ E   An **ace** with a knife, cutting an eel. Or, an ape jumps into a sea full of knives to catch an eel.

B—B D♯ F♯   A **bed** being cut by half a knife. Or, a gigantic bean is being cut by a dean with half a knife. Or, a gigantic bean is **deaf**; it has a knife stuck into each ear.

Once you know the major chords, you almost automatically know the sharp and flat chords. In writing, a major note is flatted by adding the flat symbol (♭) to it, which lowers it slightly—B♭ is lower than B but not quite an A. A sharp note is flatted by simply removing the sharp symbol. A major note is sharped by adding the sharp symbol, and a sharp note is sharped by adding another sharp. The symbol for a double sharp is ✕.

So. If you already know that a D chord is D F♯ A, a D-flat chord is D♭ F A♭ (you've flatted *each* note); a D-sharp chord is D♯F✕A♯ (you've sharped each note). Musicians have told us that our systems come in handy for remembering chord progressions. Once you know how to picture a chord, you can form a Link to remind you of the progression (sequence) of chords for any piece of music. Amateurs who play for their own and others' entertainment—often "by ear," or without reading music—find the systems particularly useful.

One student who played piano in a nightclub lounge years

ago had an interesting gimmick. Whenever *any* published song title was called, he'd play the song. There are many thousands of songs, and he knew them all—all he needed was a reminder of the first four or so notes. Once he played those, his fingers automatically played the rest of the melody. His memory problem —"How do I associate the title of a song to the first few notes?"—had been solved by assigning a number to each note on the staff. One glance at the following diagram will make this clear:

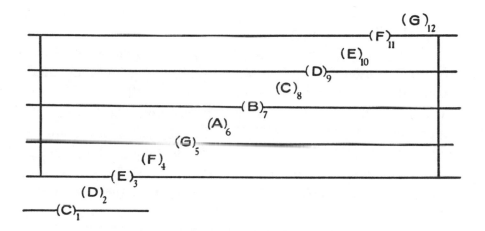

Once you familiarize yourself with the notes, locations, and numbers, the solution is obvious. Any four notes will transpose to a four-digit number; any seven notes will transpose to a seven-digit number. And—you already know how to memorize numbers.

The first seven notes of "Mary Had a Little Lamb," played in the key of C, are EDCDEEE. Look at the diagram, and you'll see that these notes transpose to 3212333. An association of a **lamb** on a **mountain** would remind you of the first four notes. If you needed a reminder of all seven, you might see that lamb on a mountain, singing "My Mammy." Any words that give you the proper numbers phonetically will do.

The association will remind you of the two things you need to know—the title and the first few notes. One more example: The first seven notes of "Begin the Beguine" are CDEGEDE, and they transpose to 1235323. Picture a **tin mule beginning** something, and you have your reminder of the first four notes. (A **bee** drinking **gin,** a **big inn,** or **beak in** would also remind you of the song title.) To remember the first seven notes, you might use **tin mule my name.**

As usual, it is the idea that's important, not the Key Word you select or the phrase you make up for the numbers. If the Key Word reminds you of the title and the word or phrase fits phonetically, the system will work.

If you're at all familiar with the music staff, knowing which number represents which note is a matter of a few moments' concentration. If you need some help, apply the systems. An association of Alphabet Word to Peg Word will do it instantly. Associate sea to tie, dean to Noah, eel to Ma, half to rye, jeans to law, ape to shoe, and bean to cow. To distinguish the octaves, you might then associate sea to hive, dean to bay, eel to tease, half to tote, and sea to ton. (You'd know that the words that are *not* basic Peg Words represent the higher octave notes.)

If you've read up to this point, and understand how the systems apply, then you obviously know more about music than we do, and you'll be able to patternize the ideas to fit your particular problem.

On a basic beginner's (six-string) guitar there are twelve frets. While learning the fundamentals, you'd rarely go past the third fret. In playing a particular note, the basic memory problem would be to know, or remember, which finger presses which string at which fret. This diagram shows the notes for open strings (no finger pressing down on any string):

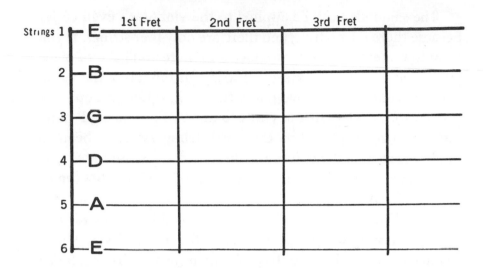

To produce a high C, you'd press your first finger on the second (B) string at the first fret. Always think in that order: finger, string, fret. An association of sea (C) to **tent** would give you the information. You don't really need the last digit—at the beginning, the finger and fret digits are the same—so **tin** would suffice. You'd know that the first digit tells you finger *and* fret.

To play a high G, you'd press your third finger on the first string at the third fret; see a pair of **jeans** (G) being a door **mat**. For low C: third finger, fifth string, third fret; associate **low sea** to **mule**. For middle E: second finger, fourth string, second fret; associate **eel** to **Nero**.

As usual, there's another way to handle it; for low C, you could simply associate **sea** to **camel**; or, you could just think **camel**. The first letter tells you the note, and the next two consonant sounds tell you finger and string. All that remains is for you to decide on a standard picture for high, low, and middle, and you're on your way. (If you know the strings by note, you can use the letter to represent the string; for high C, associate **sea** to **tub**—first finger, B string.)

The same idea can be applied to the violin; it's even easier because there are no frets, and there are only four strings. If you want to remember that to produce an F note you have to place your second finger on the second string (at the top of the violin neck; as your fingers move down the neck, different notes are produced), associate **half** or **effort** to **nun**. To produce a B note, the first finger is placed on the third string; associate **bean** to **tomb**. Or, as with the guitar, use one word or phrase to tell you note, finger, and string: **fine inn** or **fannin'** for F, and **bet 'im** or **beat 'em** for B.

There's no reason why the systems shouldn't work for any instrument. For example, a beginner on the trumpet would have to remember which valves to push down for which note. Since there are only three valves, the note would be associated to a word that represents, say, 12, 13, 23, 123, etc.

Of course, any instrument becomes more complicated as you progress. With a trumpet, the proper method of blowing is also essential. What we've tried to do in this chapter is to show you how the systems can make the fundamentals easier to grasp. That way, you get to the excitement—and the fun—of playing a musical instrument sooner.

23 *READING*

The term *speed-reading* is a common one, yet it really doesn't mean what it says—not the way it's being used today. People who say they "speed-read" are not really reading, they're "idea-culling." And when someone tells you his reading speed is, say, 1,500 words per minute, remember this: Authorities on reading have effectively demonstrated that it is physiologically impossible to read more than 800 words a minute!

The misconception goes deeper. When we've asked people who claim to be able to read thousands of words per minute whether they *remember* what they've read, there's usually a moment of slightly embarrassed silence. And, slow reading is usually a *memory problem.*

Most often, it is *regression* that slows you down. The very slow readers are horizontal regressors. That is, by the time they get to the end of a sentence, they've forgotten or haven't grasped what was at the beginning of that sentence—so their eyes must go back, horizontally, to the beginning. The vertical regressors are a little better off. They're the readers who will get to the third or fourth paragraph and forget what was in the first—their eyes must go back, vertically, to that first paragraph.

Don't misunderstand; there are ways to reasonably improve

your reading speed. But, in our opinion, there is only one way to read better, faster, and more effectively—and that is to read at your normal rate of speed and *remember as you read*. The goal is to be able to read any material only once, and know it! Eventually, achieving this goal will also increase your "normal" reading speed. To paraphrase educator Mortimer J. Adler: When it comes to reading material, the point is not how fast you can get through the material, but how much of the material can get through to you.

You now have the necessary knowledge to remember any reading material, *as you read*. The facts in reading material are usually sequential, so you would apply, basically, the Link system of memory. Within any reading material, you may come across names, words you're not familiar with, numbers, letters, facts, concepts, whatever. None of these need hang you up, because you've learned how to memorize them. You know the Substitute Word system, which will help you remember the names, words, facts, and concepts. You are aware of the Key Word or thought idea, which, along with the Link, will help you to keep these things in sequence. You know how to picture numbers and letters, and that takes care of remembering them as you read.

All you have to do is apply the systems you've learned to reading material. Let's assume you want to remember the facts in a news item like this one:

In the history of railroading, few tracks have been laid faster than those of the Tanzam Railway in Zambia. At this moment, it is moving from the port of Dar es Salaam to Zambia's copper belt. The 1,162-mile line is being built by Chinese laborers, with the help of a $402-million loan from China. Already completed are 21 tunnels and 200 bridges. The entire line is expected to be completed about 18 months ahead of schedule.

This news item is about Zambia and its railway, so you should start the Link with a "heading" picture, a Substitute thought that will remind you of Zambia. The one we used is **zombie. Sam be here, some be here, Sam bee**, or **Sam be a** would all do as well. The one you think of yourself is usually best for you, but we'll assume you're using **zombie** to start your Link for Zambia.

Before going into the Link, we want to be sure you realize that although we need a lot of words to describe them, the silly pictures are formed as fast as thought. All right then. Picture a **zombie walking** very fast along a **railroad track**; the sun is so hot that it **tans 'im**. This silly picture will remind you of the first few facts: You're reading about Zambia, the railway tracks are being laid very quickly, and the railway is the Tanzam Railway. Before you continue, be sure to see that ridiculous picture.

Now, to continue the Link: **There is salami** (Dar es Salaam) falling on the **zombie's copper belt**. See a silly picture of millions of pieces of salami falling on the zombie's copper belt. Salami is probably enough to remind you of Dar es Salaam but, if you like, you can see yourself pointing to the huge salami and saying, "There is salami." You can also put in an association for **port**— port wine would do. Most important is that you actually see the picture.

See the zombie's copper belt (or the salami, since either one can be considered as being the last thing in your mind) turning into a **taut chain** that stretches for **miles**. This picture reminds you of the next fact: taut chain transposes to 1,162, and the picture tells you that the railway will be 1,162 miles long. You may have thought of **dud chain, tight chin**, or **did shine**, but we'll assume you're using taut **chain**.

Continuing: You might picture many Chinese people (picture the slanted eyes, or see them with **shiny knees**) **laboring** to hold up that taut chain. Each one is getting a gigantic raisin (402) from a giant Chinese man. This silly picture reminds you that Chinese laborers are building the railway with the help of a $402-million loan from China.

For the next few facts: See a gigantic raisin running through a **tunnel** as it ties a knot (21) or throws a **net** (again, 21) around the **bridge** of its two **noses** (200). This will remind you that 21 tunnels and 200 bridges have already been completed. See that picture. (Remember that if you think up your own silly pictures, you're more Originally Aware of the information. Just trying to form the associations is half the battle—you're concentrating on the material as you never have before.) Finally, see a gigantic **dove** (18) flying **ahead** of the raisin—the railway is expected to be completed 18 months ahead of schedule.

A fast review: That dove, which is the last thing in your mind, is flying ahead of the raisin (18 months ahead of schedule) that is running through a tunnel, tying a knot around the bridge of its noses (21 tunnels and 200 bridges have been completed); a gigantic raisin is being given or loaned to Chinese laborers by a giant Chinese man (the railway is being built by Chinese laborers with the help of a $402-million loan from China); many Chinese laborers are holding up miles of taut chain (the railway is 1,162 miles long); the taut chain comes from a zombie's copper belt upon which salami is falling (the railway runs from Dar es Salaam to Zambia's copper belt); the zombie is walking quickly along a track as the sun tans 'im (track for the Tanzam Railway in Zambia is being laid quickly).

If you've really tried to see the pictures clearly, you should be able to fill in the following blanks:

What country is being discussed? _____.
What is the name of the railway? _____.
The railway is moving from port _____ to _____'s _____ belt.

The railway will be ＿＿＿＿＿＿ miles long.

It is being built by ＿＿＿＿＿＿ laborers, with the help of a $＿＿＿＿ loan from ＿＿＿＿＿.

Already completed are ＿＿＿＿＿ tunnels and 200 ＿＿＿＿＿.

The line is expected to be completed ＿＿＿ months ahead of schedule.

Even though you've made a Link, which is used to remember things in sequence, you'll know any fact without having to go through the entire Link. Try to answer these without going over the Link in your mind:

How long will the completed railway be? ＿＿＿＿＿ miles.

What is the name of Zambia's railway? ＿＿＿＿＿.

How many millions did China loan Zambia? $＿＿＿＿.

The first few times you apply the systems to technical reading material, they will slow down your reading rate. On the other hand, you won't have to spend time going over the material again and again. And as you apply the system, you'll see that you'll eventually be reading close to your normal rate of speed—and reading the material only *once*. And as your proficiency increases, so will your "normal" reading speed.

In our example, every fact from the news item was included in the Link. Obviously, when you're doing this on your own you'll be selective—you'll Link only what you feel you need to remember.

The idea is applicable to *any* kind of reading material—and the more technical the material, the more useful the ideas. As you read, you can remember the names, places, and events of a historical novel, the names and applications of new drugs in a medical magazine, the style numbers and prices in a business report, the names and legal precedents in a law journal. Anything!

If you wish, you can even remember the page number on which a particular fact or quote appears. Simply associate a Key Word from the fact or quote to the Peg Word that represents that page number. If you have no Peg Word for the page number, make one up—it will work just as well. This idea can be used to remember, say, biblical or Shakespearean quotes. The association will help you remember both the fact and the page number—and, if you like, the book title. You can associate chapter titles, section headings, or facts to page numbers. You can, for particular intents and purposes, effectively memorize an entire book this way!

24 THE MEMORY GRAPH

The Memory Graph will help you remember *locations,* as well as other information. The idea is based on the letter/number combinations often used to help you pinpoint any location on a map. There are letters down the left side of the map, and numbers across the top; when you look at the guide for a particular city, you may see "C4" next to that city. If you look across row C and down column 4, you'll find the correct vicinity for the city.

There *is* a way to pinpoint locations in your mind; a way to make them tangible. Although the idea may be extended to any lengths, we'll use a hundred locations as an example. Look at the graph on the next page.

Obviously, if you can picture "C4," make the location definite in your mind, that picture will always refer to that particular spot—the box that falls at C4. Anything associated to that box will belong at that location.

The way to make all the locations tangible is to patternize them: A word will represent each location; each word will begin with the vital letter, and the very next consonant sound (any sounds that follow are disregarded) will be the sound that represents the vital number. In this pattern, the word Ate can

	1	2	3	4	5	6	7	8	9	10
A										
B										
C										
D										
E										
F										
G										
H										
I										
J										

represent only A1—it begins with *a*, and the following consonant sound is *t* (1). The word **Car** could represent only location C4; it begins with a *c*, and the *r* sound represents 4. The word **Impale** represents I3 (the sounds after the *m* are ignored). The *s* sound represents 10 in every case. All the vital (location) words given below can be pictured, of course, so that they can be associated to other information. Take a look at the list.

The pattern makes these associations easy to remember. Go over them a few times, and you'll know most of them. Once you know the words, you have a handy tool with which to solve any location memory problem. All you have to do is to superimpose the information onto the Memory Graph, then associate the vital word to the information that falls into that box, or location.

One of our students, a post office employee, wanted to remember the name, approximate location, and zip code of every post office station in Manhattan! After learning the

A1—Ate	A6—Ash	B1—Bat	B6—Badge
A2—Awn	A7—Ache	B2—Bean	B7—Bug
A3—Aim	A8—Ave. (Avenue)	B3—Bum	B8—Buff
A4—Air	A9—Ape	B4—Bar	B9—Baby
A5—Ale	A10—Ace	B5—Bell	B10—Bass

(For **Awn,** picture an awning, a sunshade.)

C1—Cat	C6—Cash	D1—Dot	D6—Dish
C2—Can	C7—Coke	D2—Din	D7—Dog
C3—Comb	C8—Cuff	D3—Dam	D8—Dove
C4—Car	C9—Cap	D4—Deer	D9—Dope
C5—Coal	C10—Case	D5—Dill	D10—Dose

(For D1, you might use **Date** instead of **Dot.**)

E1—Eddy	E6—Edge	F1—Fat	F6—Fish
E2—Enter	E7—Egg	F2—Fun	F7—Fake
E3—Empty	E0—Eve(ning)	F3—Foam	F8—Fife
E4—Err	E9—Ebb	F4—Fur	F9—Fib
E5—Eel	E10—Ess	F5—Foil	F10—Fuse

(An **Eddy** is a whirlpool; for **Ebb,** picture ebb tide; for **Ess,** picture an ess curve.)

G1—Goat	G6—Gush	H1—Hat	H6—Hash
G2—Gown	G7—Gag	H2—Hen	H7—Hack
G3—Game	G8—Gaff	H3—Ham	H8—Huff
G4—Grow	G9—Gap	H4—Hare	H9—Hop
G5—Gale	G10—Gas	H5—Hill	H10—Hose

(You might picture a large hook for **Gaff.**)

I1—Italy	I6—Itch	J1—Jet	J6—Judge
I2—Inn	I7—Ike (Eisenhower)	J2—John	J7—Jack
I3—Impale	I8—Ivy	J3—Jam	J8—Jive
I4—Irate (Ire)	I9—(y)Ipe	J4—Jar	J9—Jap(anese)
I5—Ill (Isle)	I10—Ice	J5—Jail	J10—Jazz

(For I7, you might prefer to use **I can, I can't,** or **Icon.**)

Memory Graph idea, he memorized all that information without too much effort. Just so that you'll see how the idea is applied, here's the way he laid out the graph:

	1	2	3	4	5	6	7	8	9	10
A	Village 10014	Old Chelsea 10011	General Post Office 10001	Midtown 10018	Times Square 10030	Radio City 10019	Ansonia 10023	Planetarium 10024	Cathedral 10025	Manhattan-ville 10027
B	Prince St. 10012	Old Chelsea 10011	General Post Office 10001	Midtown 10018	Times Square 10036	Radio City 10019		C E N T R A L		Manhattan-ville 10027
C		Cooper 10003	Madison Square 10010		Rockefeller Center 10020	Radio City 10019		PARK		Morningside 10026
D	Knickerbocker 10002	Peter Stuyvesant 10009	Madison Square 10010	Murray Hill 10016	Grand Central 10017	36th St. 10022	Lenox Hill 10021	Gracie 10028	Hellgate 10029	Triborough 10035
E	Knickerbocker 10002									
F										
G										
H	Trinity 10006	Church St. 10007	Canal St. 10013				Hamilton Grange 10031	Audubon 10032	Washington Bridge 10033	Inwood 10034
I	Bowling Green 10004	Church St. 10007	Canal St. 10013				College 10030	Colonial Park 10039	Ft. George 10040	Inwood 10034
J	Wall St. 10005	Peck Slip 10038	Canal St 10013					Lincolnton 10037		

He could have extended the graph to, say, 17—but, as you can see, it isn't necessary. The way it's laid out, he knew that H, I, J *up to 3* belonged to the left of the graph, and that H, I, J from *7 to 10* belonged to the right of the graph. (In other words, the Trinity, Church Street, etc., stations are south of the Village and Prince stations; the Hamilton Grange and College stations are north of the Manhattanville and Morningside stations.) Some of the stations are listed in more than one box to show that they cover a more extensive area.

He also knew that every zip code in Manhattan begins with

100, so he had to remember only the last two digits. Knowing all this, you can see that a ridiculous picture of, say, a gigantic **tire** (14) that **ate** an entire **village** gives all the necessary information. **Ate** gives you the location (A1), **tire** gives you the zip code (10014), and **village** tells you the name of the station.

The picture of a **nun** (10022) eating **mush** (36th Street Station) from a gigantic **Dish** (D6) tells you all you want to know. (The reason for not using the Peg Word **match** for 36th Street is to avoid possible confusion—you might use that to represent 10036, if you were memorizing this chart.)

For A5, the student used this picture: Many clocks (**times**) were drinking **Ale** (A5) by the light of a gigantic **match** (10036). So you see that an association of a Substitute Word or thought for the name of the station, the vital word for the location, and the Peg Word for the zip code number are all you need. Once the associations are made, all the necessary information is at your fingertips.

Actually, this is a simplified example. The student also wanted to remember the street boundaries for some of the stations. He put them into the proper locations and included them in the association or Link. For example, the north-south boundaries of the College Station are 134th and 144th streets. He included **timer** and **tearer** in his original picture to remind him of this. The east-west boundaries are St. Nicholas and Lenox avenues; a picture of **Santa Claus** (St. Nick) or **nickels** and **lean ox** would remind you of that.

Any information can be Linked to the vital (location) word. And the entire bloc of information can be put on the graph in any way you like—the way that tells you what you want to know. For this example, the student could have listed H, I, J stations in F, G, H and kept I and J empty. It wouldn't have mattered at all. Virtually the same information could have been condensed into a 4 x 4 Memory Graph, like this:

	1	2	3	4
A	Trinity (06) Village (14) Church St. (07) Old Chelsea (11)	Midtown (18) Times Square (36) Radio City (19)	Cathedral (25) Planetarium (24) Ansonia (23)	Ft. George (40) Inwood (34) Washington Bridge (33) Audubon (32)
B	Bowling Green (04) Canal St. (13) Prince St. (12)	General Post Office (01) Madison Square (10) Rockefeller Center (20)	CENTRAL PARK	Hamilton Grange (31) Manhattanville (27) Morningside (26)
C	Wall St. (05) Peck Slip (38)	Grand Central (17) Murray Hill (16) 36th St. (22)	Hellgate (29) Gracie (28) Lenox Hill (21)	College (30) Colonial Park (39)
D	Knickerbocker (02) Cooper (03) Peter Stuyvesant (09)			Lincolnton (37) Triborough (35)

In this case, he could have used a Link of, say, **Ate** to **train at tea** and **sash** (Trinity, 06) to **church sack** (07) to **village** and **tire** to **shell sea** and **tot**—or he could have made *separate* associations of **Ate** to each Substitute Word. Either method will work.

Any tabular material can be placed on a Memory Graph. Any schematic problem, any location problem, can be solved this way. If you want to remember the layout (location) of the vital parts of a dissected animal, write them in the proper boxes, make your associations, and you'll know the layout. All you have to do is go over your vital words—you'll know where each part belongs.

You can learn the approximate location of all the states this way. A 3 x 3 Memory Graph will tell you the northwestern (A1), western (B1), southwestern (C1), north-central (A2), central (B2), south-central (C2), northeastern (A3), eastern (B3), and southeastern (C3) states. Look at a map, list the states in the proper squares, form your Links (vital words to states)—and it's done. Of course, you could pinpoint the locations more precisely by using a larger graph.

The same idea works for cities of states, cities of countries, streets of cities, countries of continents, rivers of countries, and so on. You'd use the Memory Graph only if you wanted to know locations; otherwise, simple Links would suffice.

Many people have memorized the entire periodic table of the elements (chemistry, physics) by superimposing it onto a Memory Graph.

The Memory Graph also enables you to do a fantastic number-memory demonstration. Lay out a 10 x 10 graph and then try to think up a word that the vital word for each square would *logically* remind you of. Use words that contain four consonant sounds, and try not to have any repeats of four-digit numbers. Some examples: **Ate** (A1) might logically make you think of **burped** (9491); an **Awning** (A2) is a sunshade (0261); you **Aim** (A3) **rifles** (4850); an **Avenue** (A8) is a **street** (0141); the **Ace** (A10) of **clubs** (7590); a **Bell** (B5) **rings** (4270); **Comb** (C3) a bald head (9511); a **Dish** (D6) is **cracked** (7471); an **Eddy** (E1) is a whirlpool (4595); **Enter** (E2) means come on in (7322); a **Fur** (F4)-bearing animal (9427); **Fake** (F7) means not real (2145); **Fib** (F9) and **fibbing** (8927); **Gale** (G5) and storm (0143); **Hill** (H5) and mountain (3212); **Huff** (H8) and **puff** (2198); **Italy** (I1) and spaghetti (0971); (y)**Ipe** (I9) and scream (0743); **Jet** (J1) and airplane (4952).

After you've done this for all the vital words, go over them a few times until each vital word *automatically* reminds you of the secondary word. Then lay out a Memory Graph with only the proper four-digit number in each square. Now you can have someone call any letter/number combination—you will instantly (after some practice) name the four-digit number in that square! If I1 is called, that should make you think of **Italy**; Italy makes you think of **spaghetti**, and spaghetti can only be 0971. If A3 is called, you'd think of **Aim**; aim reminds you of **rifles,** and that tells you the number 4850. The more often you perform this feat, the easier it will be for you. After a while you won't have to think about it anymore; when you hear a letter/number you'll almost automatically know the four-digit number.

You can change any of the vital words, of course—as long as the word you select fits the pattern.

This 400-digit (100 four-digit numbers) feat is virtually impossible to do without the system. It's a tough one to top. You may feel, however, that some of the stunts you'll be learning *do* top it.

25 POTPOURRI

During one of our classes, a gentleman said he had a memory problem that was driving him crazy. The entire class leaned forward to hear this problem. "I dine out quite a lot," said the man, "and whenever I'm ready to leave the restaurant, I always have to spend time searching through all my pockets for my coat check!" There were a few snickers, yet the man was serious. His search for the coat check annoyed him, embarrassed him, and wasted his time—to him it *was* a big problem.

We mention it here only to make the point that the systems really do apply to anything. We told the man to number his pockets: number 1, left front trouser pocket; number 2, right front pocket; number 3, left rear; number 4, right rear; number 5, left outside jacket pocket; number 6, right outside jacket pocket; numbers 7 and 8, inside jacket pockets.

Now, each pocket could be pictured. We told him to form a fast association of the coat check to the Peg Word representing the correct pocket—at the moment he put the check into the pocket. If the coat check was associated to **rye**, he'd know whenever he needed the check that it was in his right rear trouser pocket.

If you're wondering how he'd remember that the left front

trouser pocket is number 1, etc.—he'd know, since *he* numbered them. Or, he could simply see a **tie** in the left front trouser pocket, a long gray beard (**Noah**) in his right front pocket, and so on.

The principle, of course, is the same one discussed in the absentmindedness chapter. The association would *force* him to think—for a moment, *at* that moment—about which pocket was involved. Another way to designate specific pockets would be to make up a word that tells you the pocket. For example, for trouser pockets: **leaf** (left front), **roof** (right front), **lure** (left rear), **roar** or **rower** (right rear). For the jacket pockets, you might use **jewel** (jacket left) and **jar** (jacket right). There are many ways to patternize most problems.

●

HL: It's an "unimportant" problem, but it matters to *me*. I love books. I wouldn't dream of dog-earing a page to tell me where I stopped reading. And bookmarks always seem to fall out. So, I form an instant association as I close the book. I look at the page number, and if it's page 125 I'll see the book going through a **tunnel**. The next time I pick up that book, I know which page to turn to. Since I sometimes read more than one book at a time, it's even more helpful—I do it with each book, adding a picture for the title to the association.

JL: This really is unimportant—I'm always counting things and remembering them. It's screwy, but it helps keep my mind occupied. I may count the cracks on a basketball floor, or the number of people in the stands who're wearing red, the tiles on a ceiling, the number of steps on a stairway. I've even counted and remembered the painted strips of white highway lines—I'm sure you'll be thrilled to know that there are 132 broken white lines per mile on most major highways in forty-seven of the fifty states. Whenever I return to a basketball court, stairway, highway—I'll still know the number of cracks, steps, and stripes.

This symbol, ⟋‾‾‾‾‾⟍ , in one of the shorthand methods, means *progress*. Look at that symbol—what does it remind you of? Use a little imagination, and it looks like a hook, a cane, a candy cane, or the side view of a bobsled. Once you "see" something, associate it to **progress**. If it looked like a hook to you, see yourself pulling on a gigantic heavy hook; finally, you move it—you're making **progress**. The association gives you the two things you need, the shape of the symbol and its meaning.

The idea can be taken to any lengths. In a Chinese dialect, this is the symbol that means *dragon* in English:

It's pronounced *lohn*, which is pretty close to "loan." We worked out a silly picture, or story, that made it possible to visualize the characters making up the symbol: Someone asks you for a **loan**; you're so angry at this request that you push **one-fifth** ($\frac{1}{V}$) of the amount requested, using a **stick** (—), onto a

ladder (⊟). The ladder is so tall that when you climb it you see a cup of **tea** being sipped by a **zebra** on an **elevated** train—the tea

spills onto the zebra ⊱. The "spilled" tea reminds you that the **T**

is on its side. The zebra yells, "**Ma!**" (which reminds you of the **three** short lines). The letter **L** (el train) is enough to remind you of ∟ .

This may seem time-consuming, but try memorizing many Chinese symbols by rote—you'll recognize the silly picture story for the shortcut it really is.

•

HL: When I was a private in the U.S. Infantry, I found that at the time, 1943, the Signal Corps scheduled three months for trainees just to memorize the Morse Code symbols—another three months was allowed for sending and receiving practice. I finally talked to the colonel in charge and boasted that I could teach the trainees to remember the symbols—"in less than an hour." I was all ready to explain the simple system I knew would do the trick, but I never got the chance. "What in blazes," he asked just before he threw me out, "would we do with the men for the rest of the three months!"

•

We've touched on Chinese characters and shorthand symbols to show you that the systems apply to abstracts. Well, what could seem more abstract than dots and dashes? Yet if you patternize the problem, it's easily solved.

Here's a simple formula: R = dot (•). T (or D) = dash (–). Once you have that in mind, you can picture each symbol. •– is the symbol for A. There's no way to picture •–, but according to the formula •– is RT; the word **RaT** can be pictured and, within this pattern, rat can represent only •– and nothing else.

The symbol for B is –•••, and the word **terror** would tell you the symbol (double *r*'s and *t*'s *do* count here). The symbol –•–• represents C in the Morse (or Continental) Code; the word **torture, tartar,** or **traitor** would represent the symbol.

You can make up your own words or phrases. Here are just a few suggestions for the tough ones:

H •••• rarer rye	V •••– rearrest
I •–•• retire her	X –••– turret
Q ––•– tethered	Z ––•• teeterer

Once you've made up the words and phrases, you have to associate them to their letters. One way is simply to associate the symbol word to the Alphabet Word. Picture an **ape** (A) fighting with a **rat** (•–), and you have the two things you need—letter and symbol. For B, you might picture a gigantic **bean** (B) in terror (–•••).

Perhaps the simplest way is to use the adjective idea. **A**wful **rat**, **B**ig terror, **C**ruel torture, etc. Once you concentrate on "flat **rear tire**," how could you forget that ••–• is the Morse Code symbol for F? "Flat" is the adjective that tells you that F is the letter, and "rear tire" tells you the symbol.

So you see, no information is too abstract for the systems. If the material can be written or verbalized, the systems can be applied in one form or another.

At a racetrack, airport, shopping center, etc., if you forget where your car is parked you can always wait until everyone else has driven away—the car remaining is yours! Perhaps you'd prefer to associate the car's location (row number and letter, usually) to your car.

If you're parking it in the street, associate the car to the nearest address, or to the nearest cross streets. If you park near 57th Street and Seventh Avenue in New York City, see a **low cake** driving your car; for 23rd Street and Third Avenue, see a **new mummy** in your car. If you park near 401 Fifth Avenue, see your car taking a **rest** on a hill; and so on. You know the principle—you're forcing yourself to think of the location at that moment, and locking it in with the silly association.

You can remember a person's address in the same way. Just as you can associate your car to an address, associate the person (or Substitute Word for the person's name) to the address. If you wanted to remember that Harry Cooper lives at 401 Fifth Avenue, you could picture a **hairy** (chicken) **coop** taking a **rest** on a hill, and you'd have the address.

You can remember any formula or equation by applying the Link and using standards to represent the things that appear regularly. An American flag **can** represent the equal (=) sign (Americans are all **equal**); a **miner** or **mynah** bird can represent the minus (-) sign; ap**plause** can represent the plus (+) sign, a **tree** can represent the square **root** ($\sqrt{}$) sign, and so on.

The formula for finding the area of a regular polygon is:

$$\tfrac{1}{4} \, nl^2 \cot \frac{180}{n}$$

Start your Link with a Substitute Word for polygon; perhaps a parrot (**polly**) that's **gone** (disappeared). Associate that to a **quarter** (¼) **kneelin'** (nl^2) on a **cot** (cotangent) near a **hen** that's being attacked from **above** (over) by **doves** $\left(\dfrac{180}{n}\right)$ If you wanted to, you could see the quarter that's kneelin' looking up, to remind you that the superscript 2 is written near the top of the nl. Of course, you could have used hen, elevated train, and Noah to represent nl^2; or you could make up a standard Substitute Word for *squared*.

See a phosphorous (glowing) ham reciting a poem (**Ham Poem**) to help you remember that the formula for phosphorous acid is H_3Po_3. Associate **pyre Vic** or **pie rude Vic** to **Come Hear Sam** or **Comb Hair Some** to remind you of the formula for pyruvic acid: $C_3H_4O_3$.

When you drive into a gas station to ask directions, the first thing you usually hear is, "You can't miss it." Then, you know you're in trouble! But you don't have to be—you can use the Link to remember directions. First, you need a standard for right and left. You might use a punch (**right** uppercut) and the red Communist flag (**left**). Then, form a Link as you hear the directions.

If you're told to go to the 2nd light, immediately picture **Noah** (man with long beard). Make a right turn: You're punching (right) Noah in the mouth. Go to the 4th light: You're punching a gigantic bottle of **rye**. Turn left: A gigantic bottle of rye is waving a red flag (left). And so on. Try it—you won't get lost nearly as often.

Many computer codes are really simple number codes. For a particular business, the digit 1 may represent "male," the digit 2 may represent "female," the digit 3 may represent "earns over $8,000." If a computer operator punches one wrong digit, it could cost the company a lot of money to straighten out the error. An association of digit (Peg Word) to what that digit represents solves the problem. An association of **Ma** to **faces Sue** might be all the operator needs to remember that digit and fact.

Are you a dieter? If you are, it's easier to keep track of what you're supposed to eat if you know how many calories (or carbohydrates, or both) are contained in certain quantities of particular foods. If you associate a fried egg to **disease**, you'll always remember that a fried egg contains 100 calories. Associating mayonnaise to **bone** will remind you that a tablespoon of mayonnaise contains 92 calories, and so on.

There is no limit to the examples we could include. If the problem is one of memory, the systems apply. They can help you remember *anything* you want to remember.

26 *LOOK, I'M A GENIUS!*

HL: Renée and I were flying to Washington, and I was tired—I'd done seven appearances in a five-day period. I said to my wife, "I hope it's a small audience." It had become a running gag with us, because I always remembered every name in the audience, and sometimes I didn't really feel like working very hard.

At our hotel, Renée went to check out the room where I'd be appearing, and I took a nap. When I woke up she told me, "Relax, Harry—it's really a small audience."

When I went to the room to start meeting the people for my performance, I saw what she meant. I was appearing for a group called "The Little People of America"—it was an association of midgets!

JL: That's a small audience, all right.

HL: There were about three hundred of them, and it's the first time in my life—I'm five feet six—that I ever felt like Gulliver

JL: Too bad I wasn't with you—they'd have come up to my kneecap.

HL: There's a punch line to the story. They all had special stools at their tables, so they could reach the food. I met them all during dinner, and after the dessert, I was introduced. I always begin by asking the "few" people I've met to stand up. Well, they all stood

229

up—and they all disappeared! I was staring at a roomful of white tablecloths.

JL: You mean, when they stood up they were all below table level!

HL: That's it. They started to peek over the tabletops, and we all laughed for something like five minutes. Finally, one of them called out, "You really are amazing, Mr. Lorayne. That's the first time anyone's ever made a whole audience disappear!"

•

You may not be able to make an entire audience disappear, but there are many "amazing" feats you can perform, using the systems you've learned in this book.

Take the "missing-card" stunt described in the card chapter—it actually derives from a "missing-number" stunt, which, if performed with numbers, has the same effect. Have someone number a paper from 1 to 50, or 100. Tell him to circle any five numbers. Then ask him to call all the remaining numbers and cross them out as they're called. He's to do this haphazardly, and as quickly as he likes.

You can be across the room while this is done; you don't, of course, look at the paper. When all but the circled numbers have been crossed out, you tell your friend which numbers he circled! The principle is exactly the same as for the "missing" cards; except for this you mutilate the basic Peg Word for each called number. When he's finished, go over the Peg Words mentally (from 1 to 50, or 1 to 100), and any one that's not mutilated in your mind has to be a circled number. If you know the Peg Words well, and your friend crosses out and calls the numbers quickly, this is an impressive memory demonstration.

If you know the Card Words, try this for a group of at least eight people: Let someone shuffle a deck of cards. Then spread the deck *face up*, and, as you approach one person at a time, let each one take any two cards. As each person takes the two cards, you form a ridiculous picture between the two Card Words. For instance, one person may take the 10C and the 7S. See a silly picture of a large **case** wearing **socks**. Another person takes the 3C and the AH; see yourself **comb**ing your hair with a **hat**, or you're wearing a gigantic comb instead of a hat. The idea is to do this quickly with each person's two cards.

When all the people have two cards each (you can do this stunt with up to twenty-six people, of course, but it's just as effective with ten or fifteen), ask each one to remember his or her cards and to hold them face down.

You now have a choice of effects. You can have anybody call out one of their cards—you instantly name the other one. Easy, of course; if someone calls the 10C, you think of **case**. That should make you think of **sock** (7S).

Or, you can have one member of the audience collect all the pairs of cards and shuffle them thoroughly. Now, make it look like a mind-reading stunt; spread the cards face up and let anyone take out *one* of his cards. Ask him to think of his second card. Then, with a great show of concentration, remove it and hand it to him. Same thing; if he removes the 3C you'll immediately think of **comb**, and that makes you think of **hat**. So, you remove the AH.

You can take this idea to many lengths. As one final example, you can take *one* card from each person, and mix them. Hold them face down and distribute them, haphazardly, one card to each member of your audience. Each person holds his two cards face up. Now, if you know the people by name (which you should, if you've applied what you learned in the section on names and faces), you can amaze them by rapidly giving instructions until each person again has his original pair. Something like this: "All right, Sally, give that eight of diamonds to Jim. Jim, you give your king of hearts to Al. Sally, take the four of spades from Harry and give it to Sue in exchange for her six of clubs. . . ." Once you've associated the pairs of cards originally taken by each person, you can perform many different card-memory feats.

Another card-oriented memory stunt: Let as many people as you like take one card. Each person quickly calls his or her card, plus any silly hiding place. For example, someone may say, "The four of diamonds, under the ashtray." All you have to do is to associate the Card Word to the hiding place. In this case, you might see a gigantic ashtray being a **door**. Do this with each call. Now, if someone calls a card, you can instantly tell where it's hidden. If someone calls a hiding place, you can just as instantly tell which card is hidden there.

Letter a paper from A to Z. Ask your audience to call out any letter, followed by a three-digit number to be written next to that letter. If someone calls the letter L and the number 489, form an association of an **elf** on a **roof** flying up. The letter P is called, plus the number 541; see a gigantic **pea** being caught with a lariat, or a gigantic pea being **lured**. Once every letter has been given a number, if you've made good clear associations you should know the number if a letter is called, and vice versa. This is impressive because you're remembering entities that most people can't remember—letters and numbers.

You must know your Alphabet Words, and you have to be able to make up words or phrases for three-digit numbers quickly. Your basic Peg Words and the "coupling idea" can help you with this. Make up a word that can couple easily with another word, one for each digit from 0 to 9. Here's a suggestion for each: 0—hose; 1—wet; 2—on; 3—my; 4—hairy; 5—ill; 6—ashy; 7—hack; 8—wave; 9—happy.

Decide on the word, and how to picture it. Once you've done that, you can instantly remember a three-digit number: If 017 is called, you'd picture a **tack** (Peg Word for 17) wearing **hose**. If

191 is called, see a **wet bat**. Here's one example for each "coupling" word. For 236, picture yourself putting a **match on** something; for 619, see a **tub** turning to **ash** as it burns; for 752, see yourself **hack**ing a **lion** with an ax; for 847, see a gigantic **rock wav**ing at you; for 972, see a gigantic **coin** laughing (**happy**).

Use the same kind of picture with any Peg Word. In other words, for any three-digit number starting with 7, you'd always see the Peg Word (for the last two digits) being **hack**ed with an ax; for any number that starts with a 4, see the Peg Word covered with **hair**, and so on.

Now you see that if L-489 is called, you can picture a **hairy** watch **fob** on an **elf**; for P-541, you'd associate an **ill rod** (fishing or curtain, whichever you're using) to a **pea**. This letter-number stunt, incidentally, is just as impressive if done with half the alphabet, A to M.

A really impressive memory feat is to memorize the highlights of every page in an entire magazine. Simply associate the Peg Word for each page number to the outstanding stories or photographs on that page. If the magazine contains more than a hundred pages, make up Peg Words to fit.

Once you've made your associations, you should be able to rattle off the highlights for any page number called. You'll even know the positions of the photos, without making an effort to remember them. Each association will conjure up a mental picture of that entire page. It's the closest thing to a photographic memory—try it, and you'll see!

If you have a friend or relative who has learned the phonetic alphabet and who is willing to sit home at the telephone while you're out having a good time, you can perform a fascinating demonstration in "thought transference." Tell your audience that you know someone who can actually read thoughts from miles away. Give the audience the "medium's" phone number before you begin the demonstration.

Now, have someone write any three-digit number on a large piece of cardboard—"Make it difficult," you say. "Don't repeat any digits." Everyone looks at the number and concentrates on it. Ask someone to dial the telephone number you gave before the three-digit number was even thought of. As the person reaches for the phone, you say, "Oh, and ask for Mr. Jones." When the person asks to speak with Mr. Jones, Mr. Jones will tell him that he's thinking of the number 620, and he'll be correct! How? Because of the name, **Jones**! You will have made up any name that codes the three digits (via the phonetic alphabet) to your assistant!

The reason you tell your audience to "make it difficult" and not repeat any digits is because it's easier to come up with a name that way. It's easy to come up with a legitimate-sounding name in any case; "Lorayne" would code 542 and "Lucas" would code 570, but the name you use need not contain *only* three consonant sounds.

Since your assistant knows that you'll always ask for *three* digits, he or she will ignore any consonant sound after the first three. So, if he hears someone ask for Mr. **Cooper**berg, he knows that the three digits are 794—he ignores "berg." The name **Bent**avagnia codes 921. There is no three-digit number that should cause any trouble. And you have plenty of time to think of a name while everyone else is concentrating on the number.

The "medium" should not blurt out the number. It should be given hesitantly, as if he or she were really receiving the number via mental telepathy. He might give the last digit first, then the first, and finally the center digit—we'll leave the showmanship to you.

The same idea can be used with playing cards. If you tell a member of the audience to call and ask for Mr. Sanders, that codes the 2S. The first letter always tells the suit, and the next consonant sound tells the value. The name **Haggett** would code the 7H, **C**avanaugh the 8C, and so on.

You can't, of course, repeat either of these demonstrations for the same people—you'd have to tell them to ask to speak to a different "medium," which would look suspicious. If you're asked to repeat the stunt, claim mental fatigue!

We've just shown you how to use the systems to perform a few "amazing" feats. If you've learned and applied the systems throughout the book, you must realize that there is really no limit to the feats you can perform, provided you enjoy doing them and have a willing audience. Just use your imagination to apply one system or another to whatever feat you think will seem amazing. It's fun—for you, and for those watching you!

27 FINALLY

We live in the era of the "information explosion." Each year, an extraordinary amount of new technical knowledge and information comes to light, and *you* are going to have to remember some of it.

In using many examples throughout the book, we've tried to keep them general. Hopefully, some of them are things you'd like to remember right now. But it's not important whether or not any particular example helps you remember something you need to know; what's important is that you grasp the *idea*. Then you can apply the idea to the things you do need to remember.

This is not the kind of book to read like a novel. A novel is the kind of book to read like a novel! If you've simply read through the book, nodding your head in understanding but without stopping to try, learn, and apply, you should go back to the beginning, the basics. Do the things you're told to do as you read—really learn those basics. The time you spend doing it will save you enormous blocks of time in the future.

Then start applying the ideas. That's really the only way they can work for you.